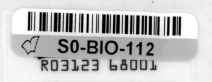

THE
REPUBLICAN
PARTY

StarGroup International, Inc.
West Palm Beach, Florida

Published 2004

FIRST EDITION

Concept & supervision by Brenda Star
Edited by Shawn McAllister
Research by Cheryl Kravetz
Book design by Mel Abfier
Cover design by Ida Perez

Designed and produced by StarGroup International, Inc.
561-547-0667
www.stargroupinternational.com

Printed in the United States of America

Library of Congress Cataloging-in-Publication Data pending.

Part of the StarGroup Spotlights Series
StarGroup Spotlights: The REPUBLICAN Party
ISBN 1-884886-77-9

Book Orders

- One to fifty copies may be ordered online at:
  www.stargroupspotlights.com
- This book is also available for bulk purchases and customized printings (interior & exterior):
  www.stargroupinternational.com
- Donations for distribution of this publication can be made through the 501(C)3 Star Foundation:
  561-547-0667

STARGROUP SPOTLIGHTS

THE REPUBLICAN PARTY

STARGROUP
INTERNATIONAL INC.

Additional books by StarGroup Book Division

StarGroup Spotlights:

- Celebrating AMERICA   2004
- The DEMOCRATIC PARTY   2004
- Understanding DIVERSITY   2004
- Saving The ENVIRONMENT   2004
- The Value of MENTORING   2004
- The Evolution of U.S. MONEY   2004
- Why Children Need MUSIC   2004
- READING With Your Child   2004
- Staying in SCHOOL   2004

Upcoming:

StarGroup Spotlights:

- Good HEALTH for CHILDREN
- Good HEALTH for ADULTS
- Healthy NUTRITION
- PARENTING
- WEIGHT CONTROL
- How AMERICA'S LEGAL SYSTEM Works
- CITIZENSHIP

Currently in Print by StarGroup:

- 101 Reasons To READ To Your Child (First Edition 2000
- 101 Reasons To READ With Your Child (Second Edition 2001)
- 101 Reasons To Be A PROUD AMERICAN (2001)

Table of Contents

Preface

"He who controls the past commands the future. He who commands the future conquers the past."
—George Orwell (1903-1950)

The study of historical events is a noble and worthy pursuit. For those among you who thirst for knowledge, this book will be a well from which you may draw many times. For those who have a curious insight regarding history, this book will be a study in politics from which to glean history and tradition. And for those who have a desire to learn the where and why of the Republican Party, this book will be a steady compass to help you plot your course.

In the following pages, you will find an excellent resource for your study of the Republican Party and the rich tapestry of its historical texture. Whether you are using this publication as a reference, or reading it for pleasure, I am sure that you will be pleasantly surprised by the wealth of information that it contains. The authors of this work bring history to life and utilize timelines, graphs, primary sources and a glossary of terms to make it easily comprehendible and interesting.

I draw your attention to the not-commonly known explanation of the origin of both the nickname, "Grand Old Party," and the traditional Elephant symbol. Additionally, you will note milestones that the Republican Party had a key role in bringing about, such as the emancipation of slaves and women's suffrage.

The idea of empowering women has always been important to me and, over its history, the Republican Party has always been a champion for the equal rights of all Americans. I believe that this book represents the spirit of the Republican Party and the principles of smaller government, less taxes, and empowerment of the individual, family values, and personal freedom have stood the test of time and continue to guide America into the 21st century. Enjoy the journey.

Carole Jean Jordan, Chairman
The Republican Party of Florida

"Those who cannot remember the past are condemned to repeat it."

—*George Santayana (1863-1952)*

Special Thanks

Special thanks are extended to Sid Dinerstein, Chairman of the Palm Beach County Republican Party, for his invaluable help, intelligent suggestions, and cooperative spirit in helping to make this study a comprehensive and enlightening resource tool about the Republican Party.

The History of the Party

The Republican Party was born in the early 1850s by anti-slavery activists and individuals who believed that government should grant western lands to settlers free of charge. The first informal meeting of the party took place in Ripon, Wisconsin, a small town northwest of Milwaukee. The first official Republican meeting took place on July 6, 1854 in Jackson, Michigan. The name "Republican" was chosen because it alluded to equality and reminded individuals of Thomas Jefferson's Democratic-Republican Party. At the Jackson convention, the new party adopted a platform and nominated candidates for office in Michigan.

In 1856, the Republicans became a national party when John C. Fremont was nominated for President under the slogan: "Free soil, free labor, free speech, free men, Fremont." Even though they were considered a "third party" because the Democrats and Whigs represented the two-party system at the time, Fremont received 33% of the vote. Four years later, Abraham Lincoln became the first Republican to win the White House.

The Civil War erupted in 1861 and lasted four grueling years. During the war, against the advice of his cabinet, Lincoln signed the Emancipation Proclamation that freed the slaves. The Republicans of their day worked to pass the Thirteenth Amendment, which outlawed slavery, the Fourteenth, which guaranteed equal protection under the laws, and the Fifteenth, which helped secure voting rights for African-Americans.

The Republican Party also played a leading role in securing women the right to vote. In 1896, Republicans were the first major party to favor women's suffrage. When the 19th Amendment finally was added to the Constitution, 26 of 36 state legislatures that had voted to ratify it were under Republican control. The first woman elected to Congress was a Republican, Jeanette Rankin from Montana in 1917.

Presidents during most of the late nineteenth century and the early part of the twentieth century were Republicans. While the Democrats and Franklin Roosevelt tended to dominate American politics in the 1930s and '40s, for 28 of the forty years from 1952 through 1992, the White House was in Republican hands - under Presidents Eisenhower, Nixon, Ford, Reagan and Bush. Under the last two, Reagan and Bush, the United States became the world's only superpower, winning the Cold War from the old Soviet Union and releasing millions from Communist oppression.

Behind all the elected officials and the candidates of any political party are thousands of hard-working staff and volunteers who raise money, lick the envelopes, and make the phone calls that every winning campaign must have. The national structure of our party starts with the Republican National Committee. Each state has its own Republican State Committee with a Chairman and staff. The Republican structure goes right down to the neighborhoods, where a Republican precinct captain every Election Day organizes Republican workers to get out the vote.

Most states ask voters when they register to express party preference. Voters don't have to do so, but registration lists let the parties know exactly which voters they want to be sure vote on Election Day. Just because voters register as a Republican, they don't need to vote that way - many voters split their tickets, voting for candidates in both parties. But the national party is made up of all registered Republicans in all 50 states. For the most part they are the voters in Republican Presidential primaries and caucuses. They are the heart and soul of the party. Republicans have a long and rich history with basic principles: Individuals, not government, can make the best decisions; all people are entitled to equal rights; and decisions are best made close to home. The symbol of the Republican Party is the elephant. During the mid-term elections way back in 1874, Democrats tried to scare voters into thinking President Grant would seek to run for an unprecedented third term. Thomas Nast, a cartoonist for Harper's Weekly, depicted a Democratic jackass trying to scare a Republican elephant - and both symbols stuck. For a long time Republicans have been known as the "G.O.P." And party faithfuls thought it meant the "Grand Old Party." But apparently the original meaning (in 1875) was "Gallant Old Party." And when automobiles were invented it also came to mean, "get out and push." That's still a pretty good slogan for Republicans who depend every campaign year on the hard work of hundreds of thousands of volunteers to get out and vote and push people to support the causes of the Republican Party.

From The Beginning

Abolishing slavery. Free speech. Women's suffrage. In today's stereotypes, none of these sounds like a typical

Republican issue, yet they are stances the Republican Party, in opposition to the Democratic Party, adopted early on.

Reducing the government. Streamlining the bureaucracy. Returning power to the states. These issues don't sound like they would be the promises of the party of Lincoln, the party that fought to preserve the national union, but they are, and logically so. With a core belief in the idea of the primacy of individuals, the Republican Party, since its inception, has been at the forefront of the fight for individuals' rights in opposition to a large, bloated government.

The Republican Party has always thrived on challenges and difficult positions. Its present role as leader of the revolution in which the principles of government are being re-evaluated is a role it has traditionally embraced.

At the time of its founding, the Republican Party was organized as an answer to the divided politics, political turmoil, arguments and internal division, particularly over slavery, that plagued the many existing political parties in the United States in 1854. The Free Soil Party, asserting that all men had a natural right to the soil, demanded that the government re-evaluate homesteading legislation and grant land to settlers free of charge. The Conscience Whigs, the "radical" faction of the Whig Party in the North, alienated themselves from their Southern counterparts by adopting an anti-slavery position. And the Kansas-Nebraska Act, which allowed territories to determine whether slavery would be legalized in accordance with "popular sovereignty" and thereby nullify the principles of the Missouri Compromise, created a schism within the Democratic Party.

A staunch Anti-Nebraska Democrat, Alvan E. Bovay, like his fellow Americans, was disillusioned by this atmosphere of confusion and division. Taking advantage of the political turmoil caused by the Kansas-Nebraska Act, Bovay united discouraged members from the Free Soil Party, the Conscience Whigs and the Anti-Nebraska Democrats. Meeting in a Congregational church in Ripon, Wis., he helped establish a party that represented the interests of the North and the abolitionists by merging two fundamental issues: free land and preventing the spread of slavery into the Western territories. Realizing the new party needed a name to help unify it, Bovay decided on the term Republican because it was simple, synonymous with equality and alluded to the earlier party of Thomas Jefferson, the Democratic-Republicans.

On July 6, 1854, in Jackson, Mich., the Republican Party formally organized itself by holding its first convention, adopting a platform and nominating a full slate of candidates for state offices. Other states soon followed, and the first Republican candidate for president, John C. Fremont, ran in 1856 with the slogan "Free soil, free labor, free speech, free men, Fremont."

Even though he ran on a third-party ticket, Fremont managed to capture a third of the vote, and the Republican Party began to add members throughout the land. As tensions mounted over the slavery issue, more anti-slavery Republicans began to run for office and be elected, even with the risks involved with taking this stance. Republican Sen. Charles Sumner of Massachusetts experienced this danger firsthand. In May 1856, he delivered a passionate anti-slavery speech in which he made critical remarks about several pro-slavery senators, including Andrew F. Butler of South Carolina. Sumner infuriated Rep. Preston S. Brooks, the son of one of Butler's cousins, who felt his family honor had been insulted. Two days later, Brooks walked into the Senate and beat Sumner unconscious with a cane. This incident electrified the nation and helped to galvanize Northern opinion against the South; Southern opinion hailed Brooks as a hero. But Sumner stood by his principles, and after a three-year, painful convalescence, he returned to the Senate to continue his struggle against slavery.

The First Republican

With the election of Abraham Lincoln in 1860, the Republicans firmly established themselves as a major party capable of holding onto the White House for 60 of the next 100 years. Faced with the first shots of the Civil War barely a month after his inauguration, preserving the Union was Lincoln's greatest challenge - and no doubt his greatest achievement. But it was by no means his only accomplishment. Amid the fierce and bloody battles of the Civil War, the Lincoln administration established the Department of Agriculture, the Bureau of Internal Revenue and a national banking system. Understanding the importance of settling the frontier, as well as having a piece of land to call your own, Lincoln passed the Homestead Act, which satisfied the former Free Soil members by offering public land grants. Hoping to encourage a higher level of education, Lincoln also donated land for agricultural and technical colleges to the states through the Land Grant College Act, which established universities throughout the United States.

Fully sensitive to the symbolism of their name, the Republicans worked to deal the death blow to slavery with Lincoln's Emancipation Proclamation and the passage, by a Republican Congress, of the 13th Amendment, which outlawed slavery. Hoping to permanently turn back the Democratic advance in the South, immediately after the Civil War the Republican Congress continued to push through legislation to extend the full protection of civil rights to blacks.

During Reconstruction, the mostly Democratic South, which had seceded from both the Union and Congress, struggled to regain its footing. Meanwhile, the Republicans took advantage of their majority and passed several measures to improve the quality of life for blacks throughout the entire Union. First the Republicans passed a Civil Rights Act in 1866 recognizing blacks as U.S. citizens. This act hoped to weaken the South by denying states the power to restrict blacks from testifying in a court of law or from owning their own property.

Continuing to take advantage of their majority, Republicans proposed the 14th Amendment, which became part of the Constitution in 1868, stating: "All persons born or naturalized in the United States, and subject to the jurisdiction thereof, are citizens of the United States and of the state wherein they reside. No state shall make or enforce any law which shall abridge the privileges or immunities of citizens of the United States; nor shall any state deprive any person of life, liberty, or property, without due process of law; nor deny to any person within its jurisdiction the equal protection of the laws."

That same year the Republican Congress also passed the National Eight Hour Law, which, though it applied only to government workers, brought relief for overworked federal employees by limiting the workday to eight hours.

The Bull Moose

Assuming the presidency when McKinley was assassinated in 1901, President Theodore Roosevelt busied himself with what he considered to be the most pressing issue, ensuring the Republican principle of competition in a free market. To do so, Roosevelt used the Sherman Anti-Trust Act, passed in 1890 under Republican President Benjamin Harrison, to successfully prosecute and break up several large business monopolies.

In 1903, Roosevelt became involved with foreign policy, supporting revolutionaries who then formed the Republic of Panama. His actions in Panama resulted in the treaty that permitted construction of the Panama Canal. In 1905, Roosevelt, who popularized the West African phrase "Speak softly and carry a big stick" to explain his view on foreign policy, successfully negotiated the Treaty of Portsmouth, ending the conflict between Russia and Japan. Roosevelt's accomplishments as a peacemaker earned him the Nobel Peace Prize and the distinction of being the first American to receive this award. Roosevelt easily won a second term and proceeded to continue to stand by his principles. Roosevelt, who was constantly bucking public prejudice, appointed the Cabinet's first Jewish member, Oscar Strauss. Then, in 1906, after reading Upton Sinclair's *The Jungle*, Roosevelt instructed Congress to pass laws concerning meat inspection and pure food and drug legislation. Two years later he placed 150 million acres of forest land into federal reserves and organized a National Conservation Conference. Believing in the importance of work, Roosevelt was also responsible for creating the Department of Labor.

Although his immense popularity almost guaranteed that he could be elected to a third term, following precedent, Roosevelt retired, allowing William Taft to become the next Republican to hold the presidential office.

Discord struck the Republican Party in the 1912 election as Teddy Roosevelt, dissatisfied with President

Taft, led his supporters on the "Bull Moose" ticket against the president. Playing to the advantage of a split Republican vote, as they would again 80 years later, the Democrats won the election with Woodrow Wilson. When Wilson ran for re-election in 1916, he promised to keep the United States out of World War I. Yet shortly after his re-election, the United States stepped onto the European battleground and entered the war. By mid-1918 the Republican Party won control of Congress as Wilson's popularity began to wane because World War I dragged on.

Leading The Way On the Issues

Some people have argued that Republicans fought to give blacks equal rights and then the vote as a way of wresting control of the South away from the Democrats. While it is true that almost all blacks voted Republican, these were very dangerous and controversial issues at the time. For whatever reason, many Republican politicians risked their careers on that period's "third rail" of politics and managed to not only abolish slavery, but eventually even established a black's right to vote as well. In fact, many blacks even held elected office and were influential in state legislatures. And, in 1869, the first blacks entered Congress as members of the Republican Party, establishing a trend that was not broken until 1935 when the first black Democrat finally was elected to Congress.

Meanwhile, Republicans continued being elected to the White House. In 1868, Civil War hero Ulysses S. Grant won the presidency easily and was re-elected in 1872. Although he seemed a bit bewildered by the transition from the military life of a general to being president, under Grant the Republican commitment to sound money policies continued, and the Department of Justice and the Weather Bureau were established. The Republicans in

Congress continued to boldly set the agenda, and in 1870 they proposed and passed the 15th Amendment, which guaranteed voting rights regardless of race, creed or previous condition of servitude. Setting another precedent two years later, the Republican Congress turned its sights toward women's issues and authorized equal pay for equal work performed by women employed by federal agencies.

It was around this time that the symbol of the elephant for the Republican Party was created by Thomas Nast, a famous illustrator and caricaturist for The New Yorker. In 1874, a rumor that animals had escaped from the New York City Zoo coincided with worries surrounding a possible third-term run by Grant. Nast chose to represent the Republicans as elephants because elephants were clever, steadfast and controlled when calm, yet unmanageable when frightened.

But, embracing a tradition established by George Washington and the Republican Party, which had gone on record opposing a third term for any president, President Grant did not run for re-election in 1876. Instead, in one of the most bitterly disputed elections in American history, Republican Rutherford B. Hayes won the presidency by the margin of one electoral vote. After the election, cooperation between the White House and the Democratic-controlled House of Representatives was nearly impossible. Nevertheless, Hayes managed to keep his campaign promises. He cautiously withdrew federal troops from the South to allow them to shake off the psychological yoke of being a conquered land, took measures to reverse the myriad inequalities suffered by women in that period and adopted the merit system within the civil service.

Not surprisingly, the Republican appeal held in 1880 when the party won its sixth consecutive presidential election with the election of the Civil War hero James A. Garfield and also managed to regain small majorities in both the House and the Senate. Following Garfield's assassination, Chester A. Arthur succeeded to the Oval Office and, in 1883, oversaw the passage of the Pendleton Act through Congress. This bill classified about 10 percent of all government jobs and created a bipartisan Civil Service Commission to prepare and administer competitive examinations for these positions. As dreary as this bill sounds, it was important because it made at least part of the government bureaucracy a professional work force.

Suddenly the Republicans' fortunes changed, and embarking on a decade-long period of quick reversals, the Republicans lost the 1884 election. But by this time the party had firmly established itself as a permanent force in American politics by not only preserving the Union and leading the nation through the Reconstruction, but by also striking a chord of greater personal autonomy within the national psyche. Yet while the presidency was regained for one term with the 1888 election of Benjamin Harrison, with the re-emergence of the South from the destruction of the Civil War the Republicans were shut out for the first time since the Civil War in the election of 1892, as the Democrats won control of the House, the Senate and the presidency.

Republican voters returned to their party with the 1896 election, electing William McKinley to the White House. His term was the start of a consecutive four-term Republican possession of the White House.

Republican Women

Standing in sharp contrast to the two existing political parties' present stereotypes regarding minorities and women, once again the Republican Party was the vanguard in relation to women. In 1917, Jeannette Rankin, a Montana Republican, became the first woman to serve in the House. Committed to her pacifist beliefs, she was the only member of Congress to vote against entry into both World War I and World War II.

Shortly after Ms. Rankin's election to Congress, the 19th Amendment was passed in 1919. The amendment's journey to ratification had been a long and difficult one. Starting in 1896, the Republican Party became the first major party to officially favor women's suffrage. That year, Republican Sen. A. A. Sargent of California introduced a proposal in the Senate to give women the right to vote. The proposal was defeated four times in the Democratic-controlled Senate. When the Republican Party regained control of Congress, the Equal Suffrage Amendment finally passed (304-88). Only 16 Republicans opposed the amendment.

When the amendment was submitted to the states, 26 of the 36 states that ratified it had Republican-controlled legislatures. Of the nine states that voted against ratification, eight were controlled by Democrats. Twelve states, all Republican, had given women full suffrage before the federal amendment was finally ratified.

History of the Republican Party Provided by the Republican National Committee.

Fun Facts and Trivia

- The Republican Party was formed in the early 1850s by anti-slavery activists and individuals who believed that government should grant western lands to settlers free of charge.

- The Republican Party is known to adopt a completely new set of rules every four years under which its convention operates.

- The first Republican platform, written at the Philadelphia convention in 1856, called for the admission of the territory of Kansas as a free state.

- The Republican Party officially became a national party in 1856 nominating John C. Fremont for President.

- Seventeen Republicans have been elected President (Gerald Ford was not elected, he was appointed vice president under Nixon and assumed the office of president when Nixon resigned); 20 Republicans have been elected Vice President.

- Abraham Lincoln was the first Republican to be elected President of the United States.

- Lincoln's Emancipation Proclamation dealt the deathblow to slavery along with the passage of the 13th Amendment by a Republican Congress, which outlawed slavery.
- Republicans passed a Civil Rights Act in 1866 recognizing blacks as U.S. citizens.
- Republicans proposed the 14th Amendment, which became part of the Constitution in 1868. The 14th Amendment states:
  - Anyone born in the United States is a citizen and has the rights and liberties as granted in the Constitution.
  - States that bar men from voting will have their state's congressional record reduced significantly.
  - Those who were loyal to the Confederacy in the Civil War could not serve in Congress unless two-thirds of Congress agreed to waive the restriction for the individual.
  - Any debts from the Civil War were declared non-collectable from the state and federal governments.
- The first blacks to enter Congress were elected in 1869 as members of the Republican Party, a trend that continued until the first black Democrat was elected in 1935.
- The Republican elephant symbol actually predates the Thomas Nast cartoon by 14 years, having first appeared during Lincoln's 1860 campaign.
- Before winning the election in 1860, Abraham Lincoln (1861-1865) lost eight elections for various offices.

- Abraham Lincoln won the presidency in 1860 even though he wasn't on the ballot in 9 states representing 1/5 of the electoral vote.

- Abraham Lincoln was offered the position of "Governor of the Oregon Territory" in 1849, but declined the appointment.

- Abraham Lincoln was the first U.S. President to receive a patent (for his floating dry-dock, patent #6469 on May 22, 1849).

- Lincoln grew a beard because a little girl wrote him a letter telling him that he would look more handsome with a beard. He was once called two-faced by a rival, to which Lincoln responded, "If I had another face, do you think I'd wear this one?"

- John Wilkes Booth also stalked Grant's wife, Julia, on the day Lincoln was assassinated. Instead of accepting the invitation to go to Ford's Theater with the presidential party, the Grants instead went to see their children in Burlington, New Jersey.

- As an actor, John Wilkes Booth knew that the biggest laugh line in the play Our American Cousin would be, "Well, I guess I know enough to turn you inside out, you sockdologizing old man-trap!" So Booth waited until that line, and then as the audience roared, he fired his gun and fled. ("Sockdolager" means anything big or otherwise outstanding.)

- When John Wilkes Booth leaped onto the stage after shooting the President, he tripped on the American flag.

- Lincoln was assassinated on Good Friday.

- When Abraham Lincoln's funeral procession passed Ford's Theatre, where Lincoln had been shot, one of the cornices fell off the building. Source: "2201 Fascinating Facts"

- The assassination of Abraham Lincoln prevented freed slaves in the South from immediately receiving guarantees of their constitutional rights. Andrew Johnson, a Southern democrat, took over the presidency during the four years of Reconstruction following the Civil War and he did everything in his power to prevent blacks from going through Lincoln's "new birth of freedom."

- The Department of Justice and the Weather Bureau were established during the presidency of Republican Ulysses S. Grant (1869-1877).

- The 15th Amendment, which guaranteed voting rights regardless of race, creed or previous condition of servitude, was passed during Grant's administration in 1870.

- The future Republican President Grant voted for democrat James Buchanan when he cast his very first ballot for president in 1856. His explanation: "I didn't know him and voted against Fremont because I did know him."

- Grant was once arrested for speeding in his horse carriage while serving as President of the United States.

- Grant married Julia Dent from St. Louis on August 28, 1848. His father-in-law was a slave owner who gave him a slave named William Jones. At a time when he could have desperately used the money from the sale of Jones, Grant signed a document that gave him his freedom.

- Grant worked in his father's leather store in Galena, Illinois when the Civil War began. He accomplished the unprecedented feat of rising from clerk, to General of the Armies, to President of the United States in seven years.

- Grant served fifteen years in the regular military, but ironically his initial offer to serve in the Civil War was overlooked by the War Department. His letter was not found until after the war was over.

- After Susan B. Anthony was arrested for casting a ballot in the 1872 election, she boasted to Elizabeth Cady Stanton that she had voted a straight Republican ticket.

- Republican Rutherford B. Hayes (1877-1881) won the presidency by the margin of one electoral vote in 1876 during one of the most bitterly disputed elections in American history.

- Hayes' wife, Lucy, was the first president's wife to be called First Lady.

- Hayes was the first Chief Executive to ban all forms of smoking in the White House.

- The first telephone was installed in the White House in 1879, after which President Hayes talked to Alexander Graham Bell 13 miles away. At first it was hardly used, because there weren't many other phones in Washington to call.

- James Garfield (1881) was the only man in U.S. history who was a congressman, senator-elect, and a president-elect at the same time. He campaigned for the presidency from the front porch of his house.

- Lincoln's son, Robert Todd, was Garfield's secretary of war.

- Garfield was the first left-handed president and could write Latin with one hand and Greek with the other – simultaneously.

- Garfield was the second president shot in office. Doctors tried to find the bullet with a metal detector invented by Alexander Graham Bell. The device failed because Garfield was placed on a bed with metal springs, and no one thought to move him. Shot by assassin Charles Guiteau on July 2, 1881, it took Garfield 11 weeks to die (September 19, 1881).

- Vice President Chester A. Arthur did not see James A. Garfield from the day Garfield was shot until he died 80 days later.

- Mississippi Republican Rep. John Roy Lynch was the first African-American elected temporary chairman of a national nominating convention at the 1884 Republican National Convention in Chicago.

- Frederick Douglass was the first African-American to receive a vote on a presidential ballot at a major party convention. He received one vote at the 1888 Republican National Convention.

- Called "the Centennial President" because he was inaugurated 100 years after George Washington, Benjamin Harrison (1889-1893) was the first president to attend a baseball game.

- The first president to have electric lights in the White House was Benjamin Harrison. When Harrison and his family went to bed, they would often leave all the new electric lights burning because they were afraid to touch the switches.

- William McKinley's wife suffered from epilepsy. He would always throw a napkin over her face whenever she experienced a seizure in public.

- McKinley was the first president to ride in an automobile.

- When he was shot, he begged that the man who shot him not be hurt and that his secretary be careful in how Mrs. McKinley was told. He died 8 days later. His wife never returned to the White House and did not attend his burial rites.

- Robert Todd Lincoln, son of President Abraham Lincoln, was present at the assassinations of three US presidents: Lincoln, Garfield, and McKinley.

- In 1908 Republican President Theodore Roosevelt (1901-1909) organized a National Conservation Conference placing 150 million acres of forestland into federal reserves.

- Teddy Roosevelt was the first president to invite a black man to dine at the White House. His guest was Booker T. Washington.

- Roosevelt was the first American and the only Republican President to win the Nobel Peace Prize (1906). He won for his arbitration of treaty discussions at the end of the Russo-Japanese War.

- Teddy Roosevelt was the first president to ride in an automobile while in office when he rode through Hartford, Connecticut on August 22, 1902 in a purple-lined Columbia Electric Victoria followed by 20 carriages. He was also the first president to own a car.

- Teddy Roosevelt was also the first president to ride in an airplane, in an early Wright Brothers biplane, on October 11, 1910 in St. Louis, Missouri the year after he left office.

- Roosevelt was the first president to travel outside the country while in office when he went to Panama in 1906 to review the construction of the Panama Canal.

- Roosevelt's wife and mother both died on the same day.

- Roosevelt started the process to create the Department of Labor. His most trusted advisor and successor, President William Howard Taft (1909-1913), signed the bill on March 4, 1913.

- James S. Sherman, who ran with Taft in 1908 and 1912, was the first GOP vice presidential nominee to be renominated.

- Taft was the only Republican presidential nominee to have two vice presidential candidates. The 1912 Republican National Convention nominated Sherman for vice president. After Sherman's death later that year, Nicholas Murray Butler was chosen by the Republican National Committee to receive the party's electoral votes for vice president.

- "Big Bill" Taft was over 300 pounds and 6'2". At 340 lbs. on his Inauguration Day, he got stuck in the bathtub and had to be pried out by attendants. He had a 7' long 41" wide tub installed in the White House that could accommodate 4 normal-sized men.

- Taft was the first president to have a car at the White House (he had the White House stables converted into a 4-car garage), the first to throw out the first ball to begin the professional baseball season, the first president to be buried in the National Cemetery in Arlington, Virginia, and, as of 2004, the last president with facial hair.

- William Howard Taft became Chief Justice after his presidency.

- In 1916, Jeannette Rankin, a Republican from Montana, became the first woman to ever be elected to the House of Representatives. Ironically, although she had a vote in Congress, it wasn't until the passage of the 19th Amendment in 1920 that women nationwide were guaranteed the right to vote.

- Republicans held their convention in Chicago, IL. five straight times from 1904 to 1920. Republican conventions were held in Chicago, Il. in 1904, 1908, 1912, 1916, and 1920.

- Warren G. Harding (1921-1923) was the first American President to visit Canada.

- Warren G. Harding was the first president to give a speech over radio. This happened on June 14, 1922, when he spoke at the dedication of the Francis Scott Key memorial at Ft. McHenry, Baltimore, Md. on station WEAR.

- Harding's middle name was Gamaliel.

- Vice President Calvin Coolidge was the first Vice President to become a regular attendee of cabinet meetings during the administration of Warren G. Harding.

- On August 2, 1923, Calvin Coolidge (1923-1929) was vacationing at his father's home in Plymouth, Vermont. It took several hours for the news of President Harding's death in California to reach the small town. Traditionally, the Chief Justice of the Supreme Court swears in the president, but he was 500 miles away. So at 2:30 a.m., Coolidge's father, a notary public, administered the oath of office to his son by the light of a kerosene lamp.

- In 1925, Calvin Coolidge became the first president to be sworn in by a former president, Chief Justice William Howard Taft.

- Coolidge was the first president to have his speeches heard on the radio and the first president to make a radio broadcast. The first presidential political speech on the radio originated from New York City and was broadcast on 5 radio stations with an estimated audience of 5 million people.

- A man of few words, Coolidge was famous for saying so little that a White House dinner guest made a bet that she could get the president to say more than two words. She told the president of her wager to which he replied, "You lose."

- Coolidge confined himself to 4 hours of work a day and took a nap every afternoon.

- Republican Calvin Coolidge kept a donkey at the White House. In fact, the Coolidges had the wildest collection of pets of any occupant of the Executive Mansion, consisting of the donkey, a goose, a wallaby, a thrush, a lion cub, two cats, twelve dogs, and several birds.

- When Coolidge was expected to attend a fair, a reporter asked if he would say anything once there. He replied, "No. I am just going as an exhibit."

- When Coolidge died, columnist Dorothy Parker asked, "How can they tell?"

- Charles Dawes (Calvin Coolidge's Vice President) won the Nobel Peace Prize for his financial plan to rescue Germany after World War One.

- The Republican Party was the first major party to favor women's suffrage, starting as early as 1896. The 19th Amendment, giving women the right to vote, was passed in 1919 with only 16 Republicans voting against its ratification.

- While serving as Commerce Secretary under William G. Harding in 1922, Herbert Hoover participated in the first successful long-distance television demonstration in New York.

- Radio coverage of political conventions began in 1924.

- Herbert Hoover (1929-1933) was the first president born west of the Mississippi River.

- Hoover was the first President to have a telephone on his desk.

- Hoover's vice president, Charles Curtis, a Kaw Indian, was the only nonwhite person to be elected vice president of the U.S.

- The Hoovers spoke Chinese whenever they wanted to speak privately while in the presence of White House guests.

- In the fall of 1932, a common sign held by hitchhikers read: "If you don't give me a ride, I'll vote for Hoover."

- Representative Jeannette Rankin, a lifelong pacifist, was the only person in Congress to vote against declaring war on Japan, after Pearl Harbor in 1941.

- World War II General Douglas MacArthur was the keynote speaker for the 1952 Republican National Convention.

- Following the 1952 convention, Republicans created a formal credentials procedure to review candidate challenges before the opening of a convention.

- Dwight D. Eisenhower (1953-1961) declared in his acceptance speech before the 1952 Republican National Convention, "I know something of the solemn responsibility of leading a crusade. I have led one," referring to his leading the allied forces to victory in Europe in World War II.

- President Eisenhower, an avid golfer, had a putting green installed on the White House lawn. He also banished squirrels from the grounds because they were ruining the green.

- Eisenhower was made a 5-star general after commanding the D-Day invasion during World War II.

- Two Republican Presidents attended a U.S. military academy. Eisenhower and Grant both graduated from West Point.

- The first president to get a pilot's license and the first nominee to travel by airplane while campaigning was Dwight Eisenhower.

- Eisenhower initiated the use of Air Force One.

- He was the first president to be baptized after taking office.

- The first president on color television was Dwight D. Eisenhower on June 6, 1955, when he appeared at his 40th class reunion at the U.S. military academy at West Point.

- Eisenhower enjoyed painting pictures, but wasn't able to draw, so he had someone else draw the pictures he painted. He also liked to eat TV dinners while watching westerns.

- Richard Nixon assumed the Vice Presidency after four years in Congress and two years as United States Senator.

- Maine Senator Margaret Chase Smith was the first woman to ever receive a vote for the presidential nomination at a Republican National Convention. She received 27 votes for president at the 1964 Republican National Convention in San Francisco, California.

- When Barry Goldwater was nominated for president at the 1964 Republican National Convention, there was some question as to whether he could legally serve as President. The Constitution requires presidents to be born in the United States and Goldwater was born in Arizona before it was a state.

- The 1964 Civil Rights Act and the 1965 Voting Rights Act, both of which were backed more by Republicans than Democrats, were reforms that the Republican Party struggled for in vain during the Reconstruction era a hundred years earlier.

- Both the Republican and Democratic National Conventions took place at the same time in Miami Beach in 1972.

- One GOP delegate's vote for David Brinkley in 1972 kept Spiro Agnew from winning re-nomination unanimously.

- Richard M. Nixon (1969-1974) was the first Republican vice president to be nominated for president at the end of his term. He received the presidential nomination at the 1960 Republican National Convention in Chicago, Illinois after having served as vice president to President Dwight Eisenhower.

- Richard Nixon has received more votes than any other politician in American history, with three Congressional terms, two terms as Vice-President, a narrow defeat for the presidency by JFK in 1960, a California Gubernatorial bid, the election to the Presidency in 1968 and the 1972 landslide defeat of George McGovern.

- Nixon was the first president to visit all 50 states and the first to visit China. He also met with Emperor Hirohito in Anchorage, Alaska, which was the first-ever meeting of a U.S. President and a Japanese monarch.

- In the Navy during World War II, Nixon's bunkmates taught him to play poker. He became such a dedicated player that he once turned down a chance to have dinner with Charles Lindbergh when it conflicted with a game. He also won a great deal of money and used his winnings partially to finance his first congressional campaign.

- On July 21, 1969, Nixon talked to astronauts on the moon from the White House by radio-telephone.

- Nixon was the first U.S. President to attend a regular season National Football League game while in office.

- The House Judiciary Committee issued three articles of impeachment against President Nixon on July 30, 1974, but President Nixon resigned before the impeachment process could continue to trial. Nixon was the only president who resigned.

- Nixon broke with tradition and established a private library in Yorba Linda, California. The Presidential Papers Act of 1978, which decreed that Presidents don't own their papers, was not enacted until after he left office.

- Richard Nixon and George Bush were each nominated twice for Vice President and won both elections; Nixon was also nominated three times for President and won two of those three elections. Bush was nominated twice for President and won one of those two elections.

- Spiro Agnew (Nixon Administration) was the only 20th Century Vice President to resign from office.

- All Vice Presidents of the 20th Century who succeeded to the Presidency won the Presidency, with the exception of Gerald Ford.

- Gerald Ford was the only man who held both the Presidency (1974-1977) and the Vice-Presidency (1973-1974) but who was not elected to either post.

- Born Leslie Lynch King, Jr., the future 38th president was renamed Gerald R. Ford after his stepfather adopted him.

- Gerald Ford pardoned Robert E. Lee posthumously of all crimes of treason.

- Ford pardoned Iva Toguri D'Aquino, "Tokyo Rose," in 1977.

- Gerald Ford was the only president to have two women attempt to assassinate him. Both attempts were in California in September of 1975. The first attempt was September 6, 1975, by Lynette Fromme who thought she could impress Charles Manson by killing the president. The next attempt was by Sara Jane Moore on September 22, 1975. Her motive was simply that she was bored. Later, she was pronounced mentally unstable.

- To supplement his income as a lawyer, Gerald Ford worked as a model, and actually appeared on the cover of Cosmopolitan in 1942.

- Only once have three Vice Presidents and two Presidents held office during one four year term: Presidents (Richard Nixon and Gerald Ford); Vice Presidents (Spiro Agnew, Gerald Ford, Nelson Rockefeller. 1973-1977.

- Ronald Reagan (1981-1989), at age 70, was the oldest person ever elected president.

- Reagan, an actor, and his once actress wife, Nancy, appeared opposite each other in the movie, "Hellcats of the Navy."

- After John Hinckley tried to kill him, Reagan said to Nancy, "Honey, I forgot to duck."

- Reagan became the first U.S. president to address Japan's legislature.

- Reagan was the only divorced president, the only President who studied economics in college, and the only President who was once head of a labor union (Screen Actors Guild).

- The only vice president in the 20th century to advance to the presidency by election directly after completion of his vice presidential term was George H.W. Bush. (1988)

- The first president to jump out of an airplane was George H. W. Bush. He parachuted out of a plane during WWII and again at age 72 while in office.

- George H. W. Bush resigned from the CIA after Jimmy Carter was elected president in 1976.

- All Vice Presidents of the 20th Century who ran for their party's nomination secured that nomination, with the exception of Dan Quayle (Vice President under George H. W. Bush).

- Dan Quayle was the second youngest Vice President to serve since John Breckinridge. (1857-1861).

- Fathers and sons have both served as president twice in U.S. history. In both cases, the names were almost the same. They were John Adams and John Quincy Adams; George Herbert Walker Bush and George W. Bush.

- Two non-elected Vice Presidents served from 1973-1977: Gerald Ford and Nelson Rockefeller.

- From 1940 to 2004, (64 years and 15 elections), only two Republican Vice Presidential nominees did not serve in Congress at any point in his or her career. (Earl Warren, 1948, and Spiro Agnew, 1968 and

1972.) All other nominees once served in either the U.S. Senate or House.

- The Vice Presidents who served two terms in the 20th century were Al Gore, George Bush, Richard Nixon, John Nance Garner, and Thomas Marshall. Spiro Agnew was elected to two terms, but resigned from office in 1973.

- When George H. W. Bush (1989-1993) left office in 1993, he became the nation's 5th living ex-president, joining Richard Nixon, Gerald R. Ford, Jimmy Carter, and Ronald Reagan.

- Katherine Ortega, only the second Hispanic woman to hold the position of Treasurer of the United States, gave the keynote address to the 1984 Republican National Convention.

- Dick Cheney is the first Vice Presidential nominee, and Vice President, to have served as both Chief of Staff (Ford administration) and Secretary of Defense (Bush administration).

- 2004 is the 150th anniversary of the Republican Party and the 50th anniversary of the modern-day civil rights movement.

- 791 people have received votes at major party conventions since the 1830s, 260 of which were Republicans.

- The GOP convention of 1880 in Chicago is the longest convention in its history, and the only one that went more than eight ballots, having lasted 36 ballots before nominating General James A. Garfield of Ohio.

- Since obtaining statehood in 1812, Louisiana has never elected a Republican to the U.S. Senate.

- There have been two sets of presidents who were father and son: John Adams and John Quincy Adams, and George Bush and George W. Bush. Other presidents who were related: William H. Harrison and Benjamin Harrison (grandfather and grandson); James Madison and Zachary Taylor (second cousins); and Theodore Roosevelt and Franklin D. Roosevelt (fifth cousins).

- Beginning in 1840, and in each consecutive twenty-year presidential administration through 1960, the incumbent President has died in office. The "Twenty Year Curse" was supposedly cast upon the presidency at the hands of an unknown Indian Chief.

  1840 - William Henry Harrison - pneumonia

  1860 - Abraham Lincoln - assassination

  1880 - James Garfield - assassination

  1900 - William McKinley - assassination

  1920 - Warren Harding - heart failure

  1940 - Franklin Roosevelt - cerebral hemorrhage

  1960 - John Kennedy - assassination

- There have been four cases thus far of Presidents who lost the popular vote but still became President. John Quincy Adams was awarded the presidency in 1824 by the House of Representatives, despite not having won the popular vote or the Electoral College vote (neither he nor opponent Andrew Jackson had an electoral college majority). In 1876, Rutherford B. Hayes became President despite losing the popular vote to Samuel J. Tilden, because Hayes had a one-vote advantage in the Electoral College. In 1888, in a much more clear-cut example of a candidate losing the popular vote but winning the Electoral College vote, Benjamin Harrison was elected President over Grover Cleveland. Finally, in 2000, George W. Bush became president after losing the popular vote to Al Gore, but winning the electoral vote.

- Seven presidents have changed their names legally; four were Republicans:

Ulysses Simpson Grant — changed from Hiram Ulysses Grant.

Calvin Coolidge — changed from John Calvin Coolidge.

Dwight David Eisenhower — changed from David Dwight Eisenhower.

Gerald Rudolph Ford — changed from Leslie King, Jr. (changed when his mother remarried and his stepfather legally adopted him).

Black Republican History

Timeline

1862

President Abraham Lincoln was the first president to meet with a group of black leaders.

1864

The Republican National Convention made the abolition of slavery a plank in its platform.

1868

Oscar J. Dunn became Lieutenant Governor in Louisiana.

P.B.S Pinchback and James J. Harris became the first African-American delegates to the Republican National Convention, held in Chicago.

1870

Hiram R. Revels was elected to fill U.S. Senate seat formerly held by Jefferson Davis.

Joseph H. Rainey, South Carolina, became the first African-American Congressman.

Alonzo J. Ransier was elected Lieutenant Governor of South Carolina before being elected to the U.S. Congress in '72.

1871

Robert B. Elliot chaired South Carolina delegation to the Republican National Convention in Philadelphia.

1872

John R. Lynch was elected Speaker of the Mississippi House of Representatives; he was later elected to US Congress in '73.

1875

Blanche K. Bruce of Mississippi became the first African-American elected to a full term in US Senate.

1884

John R. Lynch was the first African-American to preside over the Republican National Convention; gave the keynote address.

1901

President Theordore Roosevelt invited Booker T. Washington to dinner at the White House.

1920

The Republican National Convention declared that African-Americans must be admitted to all state and district conventions.

1954

President Dwight Eisenhower appointed J. Ernest Wilkins as Assistant Secretary of Labor.

1957

In September Arkansas Governor Orval Faubus sent the Arkansas National Guard to surround Central High School to prevent nine African-American students from enrolling in the all-white school. The "Little Rock Crisis" was the result of the U.S. Supreme Court ruling in Brown vs. Topeka Board of Education (May, 1954) stating that segregated schools are "inherently unequal. President Eisenhower responded by ordering the 101st Airborne Division into Little Rock to insure the safety of the "Little Rock Nine" and that the rulings of the Supreme Court were upheld.

1960

Jackie Robinson, the first black Major League Baseball player, endorsed Nixon for President.

1966

Edward W. Brooke (R-MA) was the first African-American elected to U.S. Senate by popular vote.

1968

Arthur A Fletcher was appointed Assistant Secretary of Labor; he was a candidate for Chairman of the Republican National Committee in '76 and appointed Chairman of the US Commission on Civil Rights in '90.

1975

President Gerald Ford appointed William T. Coleman Secretary of Transportation.

James B. Parsons was named Chief Judge of the US District Court in Chicago, the first African-American to hold such a position.

1980

NAACP President Benjamin Hooks was invited to address the Republican National Convention.

1981

President Ronald Reagan appointed Clarence Pendleton, Jr, as Chairman of the US Civil Rights Commission.

1982

President Reagan appointed Clarence Thomas as Chairman of the Equal Employment Opportunity Commission.

1989

President George H.W. Bush appointed Louis Sullivan as Secretary of Health and Human Services.

Bush appointed General Colin L. Powell as Chair of the US Joint Chiefs of Staff.

Bush appointed Condoleezza Rice as Director of Soviet East European Affairs for the National Security Council.

Bush appointed Kay Cole James, Director, US Office of Personnel Management.

1990

Gary Franks was elected to US Congress (CT).

1991

President Bush appointed Clarence Thomas to U.S. Supreme Court.

1998

U.S. House of Representatives elected J.C. Watts (R-OK) to be Chairman of the House Republican Conference.

2001

President George W. Bush appointed General Colin L. Powell as the Secretary of State; Roderick R. Paige as the Secretary of Education; Condoleezza Rice as Advisor of the National Security Council; Alphonso Jackson as the Deputy Secretary to Housing and Urban Development; Claude Allen as the Deputy Secretary of Health and Human Services; Leo S. Mackay, Jr, as the Deputy Secretary of Veterans Affairs; Larry D. Thompson as the Deputy Attorney General; and Stephen A. Perry as Administrator of General Services Administration.

A New National Party

The roots of the Republican party lay in the opposition to slavery, which took a variety of forms in the pre-Civil War era. Some opponents of slavery looked to political methods as a way of attacking the institution. Unable to find sufficient support in the dominant DEMOCRATIC or WHIG parties, antislavery men launched the Liberty party in 1840. Soon thereafter, antislavery forces fixed on a specific issue-opposition to the extension of slavery into U. S. territories. In 1848 this led to the formation of the Free Soil party. Although both these third parties quickly faded away, they helped crystallize attitudes on the issue of slavery. As the political climate heated up in the 1850s, the existing two-party system collapsed with the disappearance of the Whig party and the splintering of the Democratic Party. Out of this political upheaval emerged the Republican Party.

The new party got off to a shaky start. It faced opposition not only from the Democrats but also from the so-called "Know Nothings," who formed yet another party. Out of this political chaos came a new party system, dominated by the issue of slavery, which most benefited the young Republican Party. Building on a base of former Free-Soilers, anti-Nebraska Democrats, and antislavery Whigs, the Republican Party stood primarily for a ban on slavery in the territories. In the presidential campaign of

1856 the Republicans heralded their candidate, John C. Frémont, with the chant, "Free Soil, Free Labor, Free Speech, Free Men, Frémont." In a losing effort Frémont captured 33% of the popular vote.

By 1860, Republicans were in a strong position. The Whig Party had disappeared, the Know-Nothing party had faded, and the Democratic Party was deeply divided over the issue of slavery. In 1860 a four-way presidential race brought victory to the Republican candidate, Abraham Lincoln, who won a decisive majority of the electoral votes. However, the Republican victory was a narrow sectional one. Outside of the North the party carried only California and Oregon. Nevertheless, the Republican Party was the first and thus far the only third party in American history to succeed in becoming one of the two major parties.

Lincoln's victory led to secession by slave-holding Southern states. The ultimate withdrawal of 11 states gave the Republicans control of the federal government. In the course of the Civil War, Republicans abolished slavery. They also adopted a far-reaching economic program as promised in their 1860 platform. The leading measures were (1) the Homestead Act, (2) the Morrill Land Grant Act, (3) higher tariff duties, (4) federal aid for a transcontinental railroad, and (5) encouragement of a national banking system.

Republicans lead on Civil Rights Issues

Some people have argued that Republicans fought to give blacks equal rights and then the vote as a way of wresting control of the South away from the Democrats. While it is true that almost all blacks voted Republican, these were very dangerous and controversial issues at the time. For whatever reason, many Republican politicians risked their careers on that period's "third rail" of politics and managed to not only abolish slavery, but eventually even established a black's right to vote as well. In fact, many blacks even held elected office and were influential in state legislatures. And, in 1869, the first blacks entered Congress as members of the Republican Party, establishing a trend that was not broken until 1935 when the first black Democrat finally was elected to Congress.

Meanwhile, Republicans continued being elected to the White House. In 1868, Civil War hero Ulysses S. Grant won the presidency easily and was re-elected in 1872. Although he seemed a bit bewildered by the transition from the military life of a general to being president, under Grant the Republican commitment to sound money policies continued, and the Department of Justice and the Weather Bureau were established. The Republicans in Congress continued to boldly set the agenda, and in 1870 they proposed and passed the 15th Amendment, which guaranteed voting rights regardless of race, creed or previous condition of servitude. Setting another precedent two years later, the Republican Congress turned its sights toward women's issues and authorized equal pay for equal work performed by women employed by federal agencies.

It was around this time that the symbol of the elephant for the Republican Party was created by Thomas Nast, a famous illustrator and caricaturist for The New Yorker. In 1874, a rumor that animals had escaped from the New York City Zoo coincided with worries surrounding a possible third-term run by Grant. Nast chose to represent the Republicans as elephants because elephants were clever, steadfast and controlled when calm, yet unmanageable when frightened.

But, embracing a tradition established by George Washington and the Republican Party, which had gone on record opposing a third term for any president, President Grant did not run for re-election in 1876. Instead, in one of the most bitterly disputed elections in American history, Republican Rutherford B. Hayes won the presidency by the margin of one electoral vote. After the election, cooperation between the White House and the Democratic-controlled House of Representatives was nearly impossible. Nevertheless, Hayes managed to keep his campaign promises. He cautiously withdrew federal troops from the South to allow them to shake off the psychological yoke of being a conquered land, took measures to reverse the myriad inequalities suffered by women in that period and adopted the merit system within the civil service.

Not surprisingly, the Republican appeal held in 1880 when the party won its sixth consecutive presidential election with the election of the Civil War hero James A. Garfield and also managed to regain small majorities in both the House and the Senate. Following Garfield's assassination, Chester A. Arthur succeeded to the Oval Office and, in 1883, oversaw the passage of the Pendleton Act through Congress. This bill classified about 10 percent of all government jobs and created a bipartisan Civil Service Commission to prepare and administer competitive examinations for these positions. As dreary as this bill sounds, it was important because it made at least part of the government bureaucracy a professional work force.

Suddenly the Republicans' fortunes changed, and embarking on a decade-long period of quick reversals, the Republicans lost the 1884 election. But by this time the party had firmly established itself as a permanent force in American politics by not only preserving the Union and leading the nation through the Reconstruction, but by also striking a chord of greater personal autonomy within the national psyche.

A Grand Old Party

GOP's Origin

Originally, in 1875, the Republican Party was referred to as the Gallant Old Party. Sometime later, it was known as the Grand Old Party, abbreviated G.O.P, which became the nickname of the Party. No one is quite sure how it came about, but we do know it gained widespread usage after appearing in a New York Herald article and a Boston Post headline in 1884 proclaiming, "The G.O.P. doomed."

Political sarcasm was fairly rampant in America in the late nineteenth century. Perhaps the sarcastic environment in the charged political atmosphere of the times contributed to its usage, since the Democratic Party was established more than 20 years before the birth of the Republican Party. More than likely, it was an outgrowth from a popular colloquialism of the era that stemmed from Britain's prime minister, William E. Gladstone, who was dubbed "the Grand Old Man." The term "Grand Old" was fairly common slang, simple to remember, and was an easy phrase with which writers could have fun.

It's natural to assume that the phrase "Grand Old" would be a wonderful, great, and slightly sarcastic tag to label this young, new political party. However, whatever its origin, the moniker stuck and is still being used more than a hundred years after it first emerged as the nickname for the Republican Party. Although variations for what G.O.P. stands for have been tried over the years, such as "GO Party," "Get Out and Push" (an appropriate yet mocking phrase that arose during the early years of the automobile), and "Generation of Peace" (a Nixon-era slogan), most people continue to recognize it as the "Grand Old Party."

Sources: *Grolier Encyclopedia, Republican National Committee*

The Origin of the Elephant

The elephant came to symbolize the Republican Party as a result of a Thomas Nast cartoon that appeared in the November 7, 1784 edition of Harper's Weekly. Nast used images depicting two unrelated instances that took place at the time to satirize what was happening politically.

Ulysses S. Grant was considering running for an unprecedented third term as President midway through his second term in office. Journalists began equating Grant with Caesar and illustrations began appearing depicting him wearing a crown. Around the same time, the New York Herald concocted a hoax to boost circulation. They ran a totally fictitious story that animals broke loose from the New York Zoo and were roaming throughout Central Park searching for prey.

Nast combined the two events into a cartoon satire of Caesarism for Harper's Weekly entitled "The Third Term Panic," in which he portrayed an ass to symbolize the Herald wearing a lion's skin to scare away various animals in the forest, each representing different issues. The caption quoted a familiar fable:

"An ass having put on a lion's skin roamed about in the forest and amused himself by frightening all the foolish animals he met within his wanderings."

The elephant was one of those foolish animals he encountered, which Nast used to represent the Republican vote, not the party. The giant pachyderm was frightened away from its customary bonds by the fraudulent threat of Caesarism and was about to fall into a pit containing inflation, chaos, repudiation, etc. More cartoons followed in which the elephant reappeared to symbolize the Republican voter. In a subsequent Nast sketch he was shown in a trap to illustrate the way the Republican vote had been snared away from its typical loyalty. Other cartoonists began to use the symbol and it wasn't long before the elephant came to represent the party itself, not just the vote.

Republican Presidents

Abraham Lincoln
(1861-1865)

Ulysses S. Grant
(1869-1877)

Rutherford B. Hayes
(1877-1881)

James A. Garfield
(1881)

Chester A. Arthur
(1881-1885)

Benjamin Harrison
(1889-1893)

William McKinley
(1897-1901)

Theodore Roosevelt
(1901-1909)

William H. Taft
(1909-1913)

Warren G. Harding
(1921-1923)

Calvin Coolidge
(1923-1929)

Herbert Hoover
(1929-1933)

Dwight D. Eisenhower
(1953-1961)

Richard M. Nixon
(1969-1974)

Gerald R. Ford
(1974-1977)

Ronald Reagan
(1981-1989)

George H. Bush
(1989-1993)

George W. Bush
(2001-)

Abraham Lincoln

Sixteenth President
1861-1865

Born: February 12, 1809, in
Hodgenville, Hardin County,
Kentucky

Died: April 15, 1865 in
Washington, D.C.

Married to
Mary Todd Lincoln

Abraham Lincoln, America's 16th President, serving from 1861 to 1865, was born February 12, 1809, in Hodgenville, Hardin County, Kentucky.

The son of a Kentucky frontiersman, Lincoln struggled to gain an education and to earn a living. When he was very young, the family moved to Indiana then later to New Salem, Illinois. His mother, Nancy Hanks Lincoln, died when he was just 10-years-old. Lincoln worked hard to gain an education while working on a farm, splitting rails for fences, and keeping store at New Salem, Illinois.

He served as a captain in the U.S. Army during the Black Hawk War. He tried several business and political ventures and became highly regarded as a practicing lawyer. He had a successful law practice in Illinois both before and after his single term in the House of Representatives. Lincoln served four terms in the Illinois State Legislature, and was briefly elected to Congress in 1846.

He married Mary Todd, and they had four boys, only one of whom lived to maturity. In 1858 Lincoln ran against Stephen A. Douglas for Senator. He lost the election, but in debating with Douglas he gained a national reputation that won him the Republican nomination for President in 1860. As President, he built the Republican Party into a strong national organization and rallied most of the northern Democrats to the Union cause. On January 1, 1863, he issued the Emancipation Proclamation, freeing the slaves within the Confederacy.

Lincoln felt that secession was illegal, and forcefully defended Federal law and the Union. When confederate batteries fired on Fort Sumter and forced its surrender, he called on the states for 75,000 volunteers. Four more slave states joined the Confederacy, while four remained within the Union, thus beginning the Civil War.

At the dedication of the military cemetery at Gettysburg, Lincoln said, "that we here highly resolve that these dead shall not have died in vain - that this nation, under God, shall have a new birth of freedom - and that government of the people, by the people, for the people, shall not perish from the earth."

Lincoln won re-election in 1864, as Union military triumphs heralded an end to the war. In his planning for peace, the President was flexible and generous, encouraging Southerners to lay down their arms and join speedily in reunion. In his Second Inaugural Address, now inscribed on one wall of the Lincoln Memorial in Washington, D. C. Lincoln said, "With malice toward none; with charity for all; with firmness in the right, as God gives us to see the right, let us strive on to finish the work we are in; to bind up the nation's wounds.... "

Lincoln was assassinated on Good Friday, April 14, 1865, at Ford's Theatre in Washington by John Wilkes Booth, an actor, who thought he was helping the South.

Booth was found hiding in a barn and was shot to death. His co-conspirators were later captured, imprisoned and hanged.

In the years following his death, several attempts were made to steal Lincoln's body for ransom. In 1900, Robert Todd Lincoln decided that, in order to prevent his father's body from being stolen, a permanent crypt should be built. Lincoln's coffin was to be encased in several feet of concrete, surrounded by a cage, and buried under a rock slab. On September 26, 1901, Lincoln's body was exhumed and placed in the newly built crypt. The 23 people present at the exhumation, including Robert Lincoln, feared that his body might have already been stolen so they decided to open the coffin to make sure he was still there. They were amazed to see that Lincoln's body was almost perfectly preserved. It had been embalmed so many times following his death that his body had not decayed and was perfectly recognizable, even more than thirty years after his death. On his chest, they could see red, white, and blue remnants of the American flag with which he was buried, which had by then disintegrated.

Ulysses S. Grant

Eighteenth President
1869-1877

Born: April 27, 1822 in
Point Pleasant, Ohio

Died: July 23, 1885 in
Mount McGregor, New York

Married to
Julia Dent Grant

Ulysses S. Grant served as the 18th President of the United States from 1869 to 1877. He was born Hiram Ulysses Grant in Point Pleasant, Clermont County, Ohio, 25 miles above Cincinnati on the Ohio River, to Jesse R. and Hannah Simpson Grant. His father was a tanner. In the fall of 1823 they moved to the village of Georgetown in Brown County, Ohio, where Grant spent most of his time until he was 17, at which time he received a cadetship to the United States Military Academy at West Point, New York through his Congressman. The Congressman erroneously registered him as Ulysses S. Grant, and as such he is thus known. He graduated from West Point in 1843, No. 21 in a class of 39.

He married Julia Boggs Dent (1826-1902) on August 22, 1843 and they had four children: Frederick Dent, Ulysses Simpson, Jr., Ellen Wrenshall, and Jesse Root.

Grant served in the Mexican-American War under Generals Zachary Taylor and Winfield Scott, participating in the battles of Resaca de la Palma, Palo Alto, Monterrey, and Vera Cruz. He was twice cited for bravery, at Molino del Rey and Chapultepec. On July 31, 1854, he resigned from the army and spent seven years as a civilian during which time he was a farmer, a real estate agent in St. Louis, and finally an assistant at his father and brother's leather business. On April 24, 1861, ten days after the fall of Fort Sumter, Captain Grant and his company of men arrived in Springfield, Illinois, where the Governor appointed him Colonel of the 21st Illinois Infantry, effective June 17, 1861. On August 7th he was appointed a Brigadier-General of volunteers.

Grant gave the Union Army its first major victory of the American Civil War by capturing Fort Henry, Tennessee on February 6, 1862. He pursued the Confederate Army and won victories at the Battle of Shiloh, the Battle of Vicksburg, and the Battle of Chattanooga. His willingness to fight and ability to win impressed President Lincoln who appointed him Lieutenant-General on March 2, 1864, and on the 17th was named commander of all of the armies of the United States. For his next major objective, Grant maneuvered and fought skillfully to win Vicksburg, the key city on the Mississippi, and thus cut the Confederacy in two. Then he broke the Confederate hold on Chattanooga.

Grant left Major General William T. Sherman in charge of all forces in the west and moved his headquarters to Virginia where he turned his attention to the Union effort to take Richmond, Virginia. The Army of the Potomac kept up a relentless pursuit of General Robert E. Lee's troops and in the Battle of the Wilderness, had a draw at the Spotsylvania, and lost at Cold Harbor. His relentless pressure forced Lee to evacuate Richmond, which shortly burned, forcing him to surrender at Appomattox Courthouse on 9 April 1865. Within a few weeks, the

American Civil War was effectively over, though the last land battle at Palmito Ranch took place in May 12 - 13, 1865, and Confederate general Kirby Smith surrendered his forces in the Trans-Mississippi Department on June 2nd. After the war the United States Congress appointed him to the newly-created rank of General of the Army on July 25, 1866.

Late in the administration of Andrew Johnson, Gen. Ulysses S. Grant quarreled with the President and aligned himself with the Radical Republicans. He was, as the symbol of Union victory during the Civil War, their logical candidate for President in 1868. Grant was chosen as the Republican presidential candidate at the Republican National Convention in Chicago on May 20, 1868 with no real opposition. He won in the general election with a majority of 3,012,833 out of a total of 5,716,082 votes cast. During his campaign for re-election in 1872, Grant was attacked by Liberal Republican reformers. The General's friends in the Republican Party came to be known as "the Old Guard." Grant allowed Radical Reconstruction to run its course in the South, bolstering it at times with military force.

After he retired from the Presidency, Grant became a partner in a financial firm, which later went bankrupt. He was diagnosed with throat cancer and began to write his memoirs to pay his debts and provide for his family. His writing ultimately earned nearly $450,000. Soon after completing the last page, he died on July 23, 1885 in Mount McGregor, New York.

Rutherford B. Hayes

Nineteenth President
1877-1881

Born: October 4, 1822 in
Delaware, Ohio

Died: January 17, 1893 in
Fremont, Ohio

Married to
Lucy Ware Webb Hayes

Rutherford Birchard Hayes served as America's 19th President from 1877 to 1881 He was born October 4, 1822 in Delaware, Ohio to Rutherford Hayes and Sophia Birchard. He attended the common schools, the Methodist Academy in Norwalk, Ohio, and the Webb Preparatory School in Middletown, Connecticut. He was graduated from Kenyon College in Gambier, Ohio, in August 1842 and from the Harvard Law School in January 1845. He was admitted to the bar May 10, 1845, and commenced practice in Lower Sandusky, which is now Fremont. He moved to Cincinnati in 1849 and resumed the practice of law and was city solicitor from 1857 to 1859. He was commissioned a major of the Twenty-third Regiment, Ohio Volunteer Infantry, June 27, 1861, lieutenant colonel October 24, 1861, colonel October 24, 1862, brigadier general of Volunteers October 9, 1864 and brevetted major general of Volunteers March 3, 1865.

He fought in the Civil War, where he was wounded in action, and rose to the rank of brevet major general. While in the Army, Cincinnati Republicans selected him to run for the House of Representatives. Although he refused to campaign, he was elected by a heavy majority and entered Congress in December 1865

Hayes was elected as a Republican to the 39th and 40th Congresses and served from March 4, 1865, to July 20, 1867, when he resigned, after being nominated for Governor of Ohio. He was Governor from 1868 to 1872, and an unsuccessful candidate for election to the 43rd Congress. He was again elected Governor and served from January 1876 to March 2, 1877, when he resigned, having been elected President of the United States. Since March 4, 1877 was a Sunday, Hayes was administered the oath of office in the Red Room of the White House on March 3. He took the oath again publicly on March 5 on the East Portico of the Capitol, and he served until March 4, 1881.

Hayes' opponent in the presidential election, Democrat Samuel J. Tilden was the favorite to win the presidential election and, actually won the popular vote by about 250,000 votes with about 8.5 million votes total. The final decision was left to the United States Electoral College, where the votes of four states were contested. In order to win, the candidates had to have 185 votes: Tilden was short just one, with 184 votes, Hayes had 165, with 20 votes representing four states being contested. Three of those states, Florida, Louisiana, and South Carolina, were in the South, which was still under military occupation.

After months of deliberation and bargaining, Southern Democrats were assured that if Hayes was elected, he would pull federal troops out of the south and end Reconstruction. In exchange, Democrats agreed to a committee to determine the final outcome of the election. The committee, which consisted of eight Republicans and seven Democrats, voted to give all the disputed electoral votes to Hayes. The Republicans justified this saying that the problem in these states was over who had the right to vote. The Democrats felt that they had been robbed of the presidency, and dubbed Hayes "Rutherfraud."

Hayes had announced in advance that he would serve only one term, and retired in 1881 to Spiegel Grove, his home in Fremont, Ohio where he died January 17, 1893.

James A. Garfield

Twentieth President
1881

Born: November 19, 1831, in
Orange, Ohio

Died: September 19, 1881, in
Elbberon, New Jersey after being
shot July 2, in Washington, D. C.

Married to
Lucretia Rudolph Garfield

James A. Garfield, the 20th President of the United States, served the country until his death in 1881. He was in office only six months and 15 days.

Born November 19, 1831, in Cuyahoga County, Ohio, Garfield was the first left-handed President and the second U.S. President to be assassinated. He was named for his older brother, James Ballou Garfield, who died in infancy, and his father, Abram Garfield, who died in 1833.

From 1851-1854 he attended the Western Reserve Eclectic Institute, which was later named Hiram College, in Hiram, Ohio. He transferred to Williams College in Williamstown, Massachusetts, where he graduated in 1856, as an outstanding student who enjoyed all subjects except chemistry. He was an instructor in classical languages at the Eclectic Institute for the 1856-1857 year, and was named president of the Institute from 1857 to 1860.

On November 11, 1858, he married Lucretia Randolph. They had five children. His son, James Rudolph Garfield, entered into politics and became Secretary of the Interior under Theodore Roosevelt.

Garfield was elected as a Republican to the Ohio Senate in 1859. During the secession crisis, he advocated coercing the seceding states back into the Union. In 1862, when Union military victories had been few, he successfully led a brigade at Middle Creek, Kentucky, against Confederate troops. At 31, Garfield became a brigadier general, and two years later a major general of volunteers. Also in 1862, Ohioans elected him to Congress. President Lincoln convinced him to resign his commission saying it was easier to find major generals than to obtain effective Republicans for Congress. Garfield won re-election for 18 years, and became the leading Republican in the House.

At the 1880 Republican Convention, Garfield failed to win the Presidential nomination for his friend John Sherman. Then, on the 36th ballot, Garfield became the "dark horse" nominee, narrowly defeating the Democratic nominee, General Winfield Scott Hancock by a margin of only 10,000 popular votes.

Garfield was shot by Charles J. Guiteau on July 2, 1881, just a few months after taking office. Some say that Garfield's assassin was upset that he was passed over as the United States consul in Paris; others say that he believed God had told him to kill the President. Some think the "God" was a group of bankers opposed to Garfield's hard-currency policies. One of the bullets that struck Garfield lodged in his back and could not be found. Alexander Graham Bell developed a metal detector in an effort to find the bullet, but the metal bedframe he was lying on confused the instrument. On September 6, Garfield was taken to the New Jersey seaside. For a few days he seemed to be recuperating, but on September 19, 1881, he died from an infection and internal hemorrhage.

Chester A. Arthur

Twenty-First President
1881

Born: October 5, 1829 in
Fairfield, Vermont

Died: November 18, 1886 in
New York, New York

Married to
Ellen Lewis Herndon Arthur

Chester A. Arthur, the 21st President of the United States, serving from 1881 to 1885, was born on October 5, 1829 in Fairfield, Franklin County, Vermont to William Arthur and Malvina Stone. The son of a Baptist preacher who had emigrated from northern Ireland, Arthur was a graduate of public schools and earned his degree in 1848 at Union College in Schenectady, New York. He became principal of an academy in North Pownal, Vt. in 1851. He was admitted to the bar in 1854, and practiced law in New York City where he took an active part in the reorganization of the State militia.

Arthur served as acting quartermaster general of the State in 1861, during the Civil War. He was commissioned inspector general, appointed quartermaster general with the rank of brigadier general, and served until 1862. He resumed the practice of law in New York City, and was appointed by President Ulysses Grant as collector of the Port of New York 1871-1878.

Married to Ellen Lewis Herndon, Arthur was elected Vice President of the United States on the Republican ticket with President James Garfield for the term beginning March 4, 1881. Upon the death of President Garfield, Arthur became President of the United States on September 20, 1881.

Acting independently of party dogma, Arthur tried to lower tariff rates so the Government would not be embarrassed by annual surpluses of revenue. Congress raised about as many rates as it trimmed, but Arthur signed the Tariff Act of 1883. Aggrieved Westerners and Southerners looked to the Democratic Party for redress, and the tariff began to emerge as a major political issue between the two parties.

The Arthur Administration put into effect the first general Federal immigration law and in 1882 Arthur approved a measure excluding paupers, criminals, and lunatics. Congress suspended Chinese immigration for ten years, later making the restriction permanent.

He served his country as President until March 3, 1885. A well-kept secret that Arthur had known since a year after he became President, was that he was suffering from a fatal kidney disease. He kept himself in the running for the Presidential nomination in 1884 in order not to appear that he feared defeat. But, he was not re-nominated. He returned to New York City where he died November 18, 1886. He is buried in the Rural Cemetery in Albany, New York.

Benjamin Harrison

Twenty-Third President
1889-1893

Born: August 20, 1833 in
North Bend, Ohio

Died: March 13, 1901 in
Indianapolis, Indiana

Married to
Caroline Lavina Scott Harrison

Benjamin Harrison, the 23rd President of the United States, serving from 1889 to1893, was born August 20, 1833 on a farm by the Ohio River below Cincinnati in North Bend, Ohio. A grandson of President William Henry Harrison, he attended Miami University in Oxford, Ohio, where he was a member of the fraternity Phi Delta Theta, and graduated in 1852. He studied law in Cincinnati then moved to Indianapolis in 1854. He was admitted to the bar and became reporter of the decisions of the supreme court of the State.

Harrison served in the Union Army during the Civil War. He was re-elected reporter of the State supreme court while he was in the field, and served four years. He ran unsuccessfully as the Republican candidate for Governor of Indiana in 1876. He was appointed a member of the Mississippi River Commission in 1879, and elected to the United States Senate, where he served from March 4, 1881, to March 3, 1887. He served as chairman of the Committee on Transportation Routes to the Seaboard in the 47th Congress and the Committee on Territories in the 48th and 49th Congresses.

Harrison was elected President of the United States in 1888. During the election, Harrison received 100,000 less popular votes than Cleveland, but carried the Electoral College 233 to 168. Although Harrison had made no political bargains, his supporters had given numerous pledges upon his behalf. He was inaugurated on March 4, 1889, and served until March 4, 1893.

Harrison was proud of the vigorous foreign policy which he helped shape. The first Pan American Congress met in Washington in 1889, establishing an information center which later became the Pan American Union. At the end of his administration Harrison submitted to the Senate a treaty to annex Hawaii; to his disappointment, President Cleveland later withdrew it.

A billion dollars in appropriation bills were signed by Harrison for internal improvements, naval expansion, and subsidies for steamship lines. President Harrison also signed the Sherman Anti-Trust Act to protect trade and commerce against unlawful restraints and monopolies, the first Federal act attempting to regulate trusts. High tariff rates in effect had created a surplus of money in the Treasury; low-tariff advocates argued that the surplus was hurting business. Republican leaders in Congress successfully met the challenge and Representative William McKinley and Senator Nelson W. Aldrich framed an even higher tariff bill with some rates intentionally prohibitive. Harrison tried to make the tariff more acceptable by writing in reciprocity provisions. To cope with the Treasury surplus, the tariff was removed from imported raw sugar; sugar growers within the United States were given two cents a pound bounty on their production.

Long before the end of Harrison's presidency, the Treasury surplus had all but disappeared. Even though he had cooperated with Congress on party legislation party leaders decided to abandon President Harrison when Congressional elections in 1890 went against the Republicans. Nevertheless, even amid the controversy, he was renominated in 1892, but he was defeated by Cleveland.

After leaving office, Harrison returned to Indianapolis, and married the widowed Mrs. Mary Dimmick in 1896. He served as an attorney for the Republic of Venezuela in the boundary dispute between Venezuela and the United Kingdom in 1900.

A dignified elder statesman, he died March 13, 1901 in Indianapolis, Indiana and is interred in Crown Hill Cemetery.

William McKinley

Twenty-Fifth President
1897-1901

Born: January 29, 1843 in
Niles, Ohio

Died: September 14, 1901 after
being shot in Buffalo, New York

Married to
Ida Saxton McKinley

William McKinley, the country's 25th President, in office from 1897 to 1901, was born in Niles, Ohio, January 29, 1843. He attended the public schools, Poland Academy, and Allegheny College. After graduation he taught school, then at the start of the American Civil War enlisted in the Union Army on June 23, 1861, as a private in the Twenty-third Regiment, Ohio Volunteer Infantry, and was mustered out as captain and brevet major of the same regiment in September 1865. He studied law, opened an office in Canton, Ohio, and married Ida Saxton, daughter of a local banker.

At 34, McKinley won a seat in Congress. He was elected as a Republican to the 45th, 46th, and 47th Congresses, March 4, 1877 - March 3, 1883. He served as chairman of the Committee on Revision of the Laws during the 47th Congress. He served in the 48th Congress from March 4, 1883, until May 27, 1884, when he was succeeded by Jonathan H. Wallace, who successfully contested his election. McKinley was again elected to the 49th, 50th and

51st Congresses, March 4, 1885 to March 3, 1891. He was chairman of the Committee on Ways and Means in the 51st Congress. During his 14 years in the House, he became the leading Republican tariff expert, giving his name to the measure enacted in 1890. The next year he was elected Governor of Ohio, serving two terms.

At the 1896 Republican Convention, Cleveland businessman Marcus Alonzo Hanna ensured the nomination of his friend William McKinley as "the advance agent of prosperity." The Democrats, advocating the "free and unlimited coinage of both silver and gold" - which would have mildly inflated the currency - nominated William Jennings Bryan.

When McKinley became President, the depression of 1893 had almost run its course and with it the extreme agitation over silver.

In 1898, McKinley launched the trust-busting era when he appointed several Senators and his former Lt. Governor Andrew L. Harris to the U.S. Industrial Commission. McKinley led the country into the Spanish-American War, bringing the former colonies of Spain in the Philippines and Caribbean Sea under American control, ushering America into a policy of international imperialism.

Re-elected in 1900, McKinley was shot by anarchist, Leon F. Czolgosz, on September 6, 1901 while he was standing in a receiving line at the Buffalo Pan-American Exposition. He died eight days later on September 14, 1901. He is interred in the McKinley Monument adjacent to West Lawn Cemetery in Canton, Ohio.

Theodore Roosevelt

Twenty-Sixth President
1901-1909

Born: October 27, 1858 in
New York, New York

Died: January 6, 1919 in
Oyster Bay, New York

Married to
Edith Kermit Carow Roosevelt

Theodore Roosevelt, II, America's 26th President, serving from 1901 to 1909, was born October 27, 1858 in New York, New York.

He was sickly as a young man, but through physical exercise he became a sporting and outdoor enthusiast, frequenting such areas of natural beauty as the Grand Canyon, thus setting an example that influenced many people to take up physical exercise during the urban sports boom in the early part of the century.

He graduated from Harvard University in 1880 and served as a member of the New York State Assembly from 1882 to 1884. In 1884 his first wife, Alice Lee Roosevelt, and his mother, Minnie Bulloch Roosevelt, died on the same day. Following the death of his wife, he moved to the Badlands of the North Dakota Territory where he lived on his ranch for two years driving cattle and hunting big game. On a visit to London in December 1886, he married Edith Carow. He returned to New York City, where he was appointed by President Benjamin Harrison as a member of the United States Civil Service Commission 1889-1895, when he resigned to become president of the New York Board of Police Commissioners. He resigned that position when he was appointed by President William McKinley as Assistant Secretary of the Navy, a post he held from 1897 to 1898, when he resigned to fight in the Spanish-American War.

Roosevelt rose to national prominence during the Spanish-American War as commander of the "Rough Riders". As police commissioner and governor of New York, Roosevelt made such a concerted effort to stop corruption and machine politics that leaders in New York chose him as a running mate for William McKinley in the 1900 election to get rid of him.

With the assassination of President McKinley, Theodore Roosevelt, nearly 43, became the youngest President in the Nation's history. He brought new excitement and power to the Presidency, as he vigorously led Congress and the American public toward progressive reforms and a strong foreign policy. He took the view that the President should take any action necessary for the public good unless expressly forbidden by law or the Constitution. As President, Roosevelt felt that the Government should be the great arbiter of the conflicting economic forces in the Nation, especially between capital and labor, guaranteeing justice to each and dispensing favors to none. He forced the dissolution of a great railroad combination in the Northwest, after which other antitrust suits followed under the Sherman Act.

Roosevelt steered the United States more actively into world politics. He ensured the construction of the Panama Canal to satisfy the need for a shortcut between the Atlantic and Pacific. He won the Nobel Peace Prize for mediating the Russo-Japanese War, reached an agreement on immigration with Japan, and sent the Great White Fleet on a goodwill tour of the world. Some of Theodore Roosevelt's most notable achievements were in conservation, adding to the national forests in the West, reserved lands for public use, and fostered great irrigation projects. He is considered by many to be the nation's first Conservation President. During his presidency, he established the United States Forest Service, signed into law the creation of five National Parks, and signed the 1906 Antiquities Act under which he proclaimed 18 national monuments. He also established the first 51 Bird Reserves, 4 Game Preserves, and 150 National Forests. The area of the United States placed under public protection by Theodore Roosevelt totals approximately 230,000,000 acres. His concern for conservation grew out of his experiences in North Dakota. Roosevelt first came to the Badlands in September 1883 on a hunting trip. The 24-year-old Roosevelt was bursting with anticipation about shooting a bison. This feat took him 10 days to accomplish since by the time he arrived the last large herds of bison were gone, having been decimated by hide hunters and disease.

Leaving the Presidency in 1909, Roosevelt went on an African safari, then he jumped back into politics. In 1912 he ran for President on a Progressive ticket. While campaigning in Milwaukee, a fanatic shot him in the chest, but his wounds were not fatal. He died on January 6, 1919 in Oyster Bay, New York.

Willian H. Taft

Twenty-Seventh President
1909-1913

Born: September 15, 1857 in
Cincinnati, Ohio

Died: March 8, 1930 in
Washington, D.C.

Married to
Helen Herron Taft

William Howard Taft, the 27th President of the United States, serving from 1909 to 1913, was born September 15, 1857 in Cincinnati, Ohio to Alphonso Taft and Louisa Torrey. A prominent Republican, Taft's father served as secretary of war under President Ulysses S. Grant. The son of a distinguished judge, Taft was graduated from Yale, and returned to Cincinnati to study and practice law. The younger Taft began his political career in Ohio shortly after joining the bar in 1880.

Although he preferred law to politics, he rose in the country's politics through Republican judiciary appointments. He was appointed a Federal circuit judge at age 34. He aspired to be a member of the Supreme Court, but his wife, Helen Herron Taft, held other ambitions for him.

His route to the White House was via administrative posts. President McKinley sent him to the Philippines in 1900 as chief civil administrator. President Roosevelt made him Secretary of War, and by 1907 he knew he wanted Taft to be his successor. The Republican Convention nominated him the next year.

Taft didn't like the campaign saying it was four of the most uncomfortable months of his life. But he pledged his loyalty to the Roosevelt program, popular in the West, while his brother Charles reassured eastern Republicans. William Jennings Bryan, running on the Democratic ticket for a third time, complained that he had to oppose two candidates, a western progressive Taft and an eastern conservative Taft.

Taft recognized that his techniques would differ from those of Roosevelt. Taft did not believe in the stretching of Presidential powers. He alienated many liberal Republicans who later formed the Progressive Party, by defending the Payne-Aldrich Act, which unexpectedly continued high tariff rates. Taft pushed through Congress a trade agreement with Canada, which would have pleased eastern advocates of a low tariff, but Canadians rejected it. He upset Progressives by supporting his Secretary of the Interior, accused of failing to carry out Roosevelt's conservation policies.

In the angry Progressive onslaught against him, little attention was paid to the fact that his administration initiated 80 antitrust suits and that Congress submitted to the states amendments for a Federal income tax and the direct election of Senators. A postal savings system was established, and the Interstate Commerce Commission was directed to set railroad rates.

In 1912, when the Republicans re-nominated Taft, Roosevelt bolted the party to lead the Progressives, which guaranteed the election of Woodrow Wilson.

Following his term as President Taft served as Professor of Law at Yale until President Harding made him Chief Justice of the United States, a position he called his greatest honor, one he held until just before his death on March 8, 1930 in Washington, D.C.

Warren G. Harding

Twenty-Ninth President
1921-1923

Born: November 2, 1865 in
Corsica (Blooming Grove), Ohio

Died: August 2, 1923 during his
presidency while visiting San
Francisco, California

Married to
Florence Kling Harding

Warren G. Harding, served as the 29th President of the United States from 1921 to 1923.

Harding was born in Corsica, Blooming Grove, Morrow County, Ohio, on November 2, 1865 to Dr. George Harding and Phoebe Dickerson. The oldest of six children, his boyhood heroes were Alexander Hamilton and Napoleon. His mother was a doctor.

He graduated from Ohio Central College at Iberia and became a newspaper publisher. In 1889, at age 24, Harding suffered a nervous breakdown and spent several weeks in a sanitarium. Two years later he married Florence "Flossie" Mabel Kling DeWolfe, age 30, a divorcee with one son. People described Flossie as a stubborn and old-fashioned woman who had persistently pursued him even though her father opposed the marriage. Her father's warnings proved right. Harding neglected Flossie, focusing his attention on his poker buddies as well as other women. However, Flossie's management skills helped them build his newspaper into a financial success.

He was a trustee of the Trinity Baptist Church, a director of nearly every important business, and a leader in fraternal organizations and charitable enterprises. He served as Ohio State Senator from 1899 to 1903, Lieutenant Governor of Ohio from 1903 to 1905), and U.S. Senator from 1915 to 1921. As U.S. Senator, he had a terrible attendance record, missing over two-thirds of the roll-call votes, including the vote to send the 19th Amendment, Women's Suffrage, to the States for ratification.

In the early 1920s, even before her husband was nominated by the Republican Party for President, Flossie visited Madame Marcia, an expensive and well-known psychic in Washington, who predicted that Harding would become President, and that he would die in office. Before he was nominated, he was asked if he had any skeletons in his closet that might be used against him in the race. He had a limited formal education, suffered from depression, had spent several years in a sanitarium, had a rocky relationship with his wife, had a longstanding affair with the wife of an old friend, and was a drinker in spite of Prohibition.

The Democratic candidate in the 1920 election was Ohio Governor James M. Cox, whose vice presidential candidate was Assistant Secretary of the Navy Franklin Delano Roosevelt. Harding received 61% of the national vote and 404 electoral votes. Cox received 35% of the national vote and 127 electoral votes. Eugene V. Debs, campaigning from Federal prison, received 3% of the national vote. As President, Harding played golf twice a week, and poker twice a week. He regularly attended baseball games. As Senator of Ohio he had voted for Prohibition, but as President Harding kept the White House well stocked with bootleg liquor.

In June of 1923, Harding set out on a cross-country Voyage of Understanding. His plan was to meet regular people and explain to them his policies. He was the first President to visit Alaska. At the end of July, while traveling south from Alaska, Harding suffered from food poisoning. Arriving at the Palace Hotel in San Francisco, he developed pneumonia and died in the early morning hours of August 2, 1923. Doctors thought that he had suffered a heart attack. But Mrs. Harding refused permission for an autopsy. Interment was in Marion Cemetery, Marion, Ohio. He was reintered in the Harding Memorial Tomb. Harding was succeeded by his Vice President, Calvin Coolidge. During the White House funeral, alone by the casket, Mrs. Harding spoke for more than an hour into the face of her dead husband. Sixteen months later, she died of kidney disease.

In 1963, numerous love letters were discovered, detailing a 15-year relationship with Carrie Fulton Phillips, wife of his longtime friend James Phillips. While he was seeing Carrie Phillips, it was discovered that Harding was also having an affair with Nan Britton, a flapper 30 years his junior. In January 1919 in his Senate office, they conceived Harding's only child, Elizabeth Ann Christian. Harding never met his daughter, but he paid large amounts of child support. Harding and Britton continued their affair while he was President, utilizing a closet adjacent to the Oval Office for privacy. In 1927, Nan Britton told all in her book *The President's Daughter*.

Calvin Coolidge

Thirtieth President
1923-1929

Born: July 4, 1872 in
Plymouth, Vermont

Died: January 5, 1933 in
Northhampton, Massachusetts

Married to
Grace Goodhue Coolidge

John Calvin Coolidge, Jr., the 30th President of the United States, serving from 1923 to 1929, was born July 4, 1872 in Plymouth, Windsor County, Vermont, the son of a village storekeeper.

He was graduated from Amherst College with honors in 1895 at which time he dropped the first name of John. Coolidge practiced law in Northampton, Massachusetts, and was a member of the city council in 1899, city solicitor from 1900 to 1902, clerk of courts in 1904, and a member of the State House of Representatives from 1907 to 1908. He was elected mayor of Northampton in 1910 and 1911, was a member of the State senate from 1912 to 1915, serving as president of that body in 1914 and 1915. He was lieutenant governor of the state from 1916 to 1918, and Governor from 1919 to 1920.

Coolidge sought the Republican presidential nomination in 1920, but lost to Ohio Senator Warren G. Harding. But, the Republican party nominated Coolidge for Vice-President. The Harding-Coolidge ticket won against Ohio Governor James M. Cox and Assistant Secretary of the Navy Franklin D. Roosevelt.

Coolidge was inaugurated as Vice-President on March 4, 1921, and served that office until August 3, 1923, when upon the death of President Harding, he became President of the United States on August 3, 1923. Coolidge was visiting his family home, which had no electricity or telephone, when he received word of Harding's death. His father, a notary public, administered the oath of office in the family's parlor by the light of a kerosene lamp as Coolidge placed his hand on the family Bible. He was resworn by a federal official upon his return to Washington.

He rapidly became popular. In 1924, as the beneficiary of what was becoming known as "Coolidge prosperity," he polled more than 54 percent of the popular vote. He was elected President of the United States in 1924 for the term that expired March 4, 1929. In his Inaugural he said that the country had achieved "a state of contentment seldom before seen," and pledged himself to maintain the status quo. In subsequent years he twice vetoed farm relief bills, and killed a plan to produce cheap Federal electric power on the Tennessee River.

Coolidge made use of the new medium of radio and made radio history several times while president: his inauguration was the first presidential inauguration broadcast on radio, on February 12, 1924 he became the first President of the United States to deliver a political speech on radio and on February 22 he also became the first to deliver such a speech from the White House.

As President, Coolidge demonstrated his determination to preserve the old moral and economic precepts amid the material prosperity, which many Americans were enjoying. He refused to use Federal economic power to check the growing boom or to improve the depressed condition of agriculture and certain industries. His first message to Congress in December 1923 called for isolation in foreign policy, and for tax cuts, economy, and limited aid to farmers.

Both his dry Yankee wit and his frugality with words became legendary. His wife, Grace Goodhue Coolidge, said that a young woman sitting next to Coolidge at a dinner party confided to him she had bet she could get at least three words of conversation from him. Without looking at her he quietly retorted, "You lose." And in 1928, while vacationing in the Black Hills of South Dakota, he issued the most famous of his laconic statements, "I do not choose to run for President in 1928."

He served as chairman of the Nonpartisan Railroad Commission and as honorary president of the Foundation of the Blind. He died at "The Beeches," Northampton, Massachusetts, January 5, 1933. Interment is in Notch Cemetery, Plymouth, Vermont.

Herbert Hoover

Thirty-First President
1929-1933

Born: August 10, 1874 in
West Branch, Iowa

Died: October 20, 1964 in New York,
New York

Married to
Lou Henry Hoover

Herbert Clark Hoover, America's 31st President, serving from 1929 to 1933, was born the son of a Quaker blacksmith Jesse Hoover and his wife Hulda Minthorn, on August 10, 1874 in West Branch, Iowa. His father died in 1880 and his mother in 1884.

Orphaned in the summer of 1885 eleven-year-old Bert Hoover headed west to Oregon where he spent the next six years with his Uncle John Minthorn, a doctor and school superintendent. Hoover's time in Oregon taught him self-reliance. He worked as an office boy in his uncle's Oregon Land Company and spent his evenings at business school, learning bookkeeping and typing. In the fall of 1891 he entered Leland Stanford Junior University when it opened at Palo Alto, California. There he managed the baseball and football teams, started a laundry and ran a lecture agency. He was elected student body treasurer and eliminated a student-government debt of $2,000. He earned his way through school by typing for Professor John Casper Branner, who helped him get a summer job mapping the terrain in Arkansas' Ozark Mountains. It was in Branner's geology lab that he met Lou Henry, a banker's daughter born in Waterloo, Iowa, in 1874. Lou shared his love of the outdoors and self-reliant nature.

He graduated as a mining engineer three months before his 21st birthday in May 1895. In 1899 he married Lou Henry and they went to China, where he worked for a private corporation as China's leading engineer. In June 1900 the Boxer Rebellion caught the Hoovers in Tianjin and for almost a month the settlement was under heavy fire. While Lou worked in the hospitals, Hoover directed the building of barricades, and once risked his life rescuing Chinese children.

On August 3, 1914 Hoover received an urgent request for help from U.S. Ambassador to Britain Walter Hines Page to help an estimated 120,000 Americans who were trapped in Europe after the assassination of Austrian Archduke Franz Ferdinand. World War I was at hand. Within 24 hours, 500 volunteers were assembled and the grand ballroom of the Savoy Hotel was turned into a vast canteen and distribution center for food, clothing, steamer tickets and cash. During the next few weeks Hoover helped Americans get home. Together with nine engineer friends he loaned desperate travelers $1.5 million; all but $400 was returned, confirming the Great Engineer's faith in the American character.

After the United States entered the war, President Wilson appointed Hoover head of the Food Administration where he cut consumption of foods needed overseas, avoided rationing at home, and still kept the Allies fed. After the Armistice, Hoover, a member of the Supreme Economic Council and head of the American Relief Administration, organized shipments of food for starving millions in central Europe. He extended aid to famine-stricken Soviet Russia in 1921. After serving as Secretary of Commerce under Presidents Warren G. Harding and Calvin Coolidge, and leading relief efforts in the wake of the Great Mississippi Flood of 1927, Hoover became the Republican Presidential nominee in 1928. Since 1930, the Hoover administration had seldom let a month go by without public announcements that the worst of the economic downturn was over, although the first was on December 3, 1929. Such proclamations were followed by more stock-market falls and rises in unemployment proving these assessments wrong. Hoover became the scapegoat for the Great Depression, and shanty towns of unemployed rising across the country became known as Hoovervilles. Hoover called for construction of a dam on the Colorado River, a 12-year project aimed at providing jobs and electricity, and generate income to stimulate the economy.

Hoover was badly defeated in the 1932 presidential election. After Franklin Roosevelt assumed the presidency, Hoover became a critic of the New Deal, warning against tendencies toward statism. In 1947, President Harry S. Truman appointed Hoover to a commission, which elected him chairman, to reorganize the executive departments. He was appointed chairman of a similar commission by President Eisenhower in 1953. Many economies resulted from both commissions' recommendations. Through the years, Hoover wrote numerous articles and books, one of which he was working on when he died from intestinal cancer in New York City on October 20, 1964 at the age of 90.

Dwight D. Eisenhower

Thirty-Fourth President
1953-1961

Born: October 14, 1890 in
Denison, Texas

Died: March 28, 1969 in
Washington, D.C.

Married to
Mamie Geneva Doud Eisenhower

Dwight D. Eisenhower, the 34th President of the United States, served from 1953 to 1961. He was born on October 14, 1890 in Denison, Texas, the third of David Jacob and Ida Elizabeth Stover Eisenhower's seven sons. The Eisenhowers were of German descent, but had lived in America since the 18th century. The family moved to Abilene, Kansas, in 1892. Eisenhower graduated from Abilene High School in 1909 and he worked at Belle Springs Creamery from 1909 to 1911.

Eisenhower excelled in sports in high school, and received an appointment to West Point in June, 1911 where he graduated in 1915. While he was stationed in Texas as a second lieutenant, he met Mamie Geneva Doud, (1896-1979), of Denver, Colorado. They were married on July 1, 1916. They had two children, Doud Dwight Eisenhower (1917-1921), and John Sheldon Doud Eisenhower (born 1922). John Eisenhower served in the United States Army, then became an author and served as U.S. Ambassador to Belgium. One of John Eisenhower's sons, David Eisenhower, married Richard Nixon's daughter Julie in 1968.

Eisenhower served with the infantry until 1918 at camps in Texas and Georgia. He then served with the Tank Corps from 1918 to 1922 at Camp Meade, Maryland. He was promoted to Captain in 1917 and Major in 1920. In 1922 he was assigned as executive officer to General Fox Conner in the Panama Canal Zone, where he served until 1924. In 1925 and 1926 he attended the Command and General Staff School at Fort Leavenworth, Kansas, and then served as a battalion commander, at Fort Benning, Georgia, until 1927. In his early Army career, he served under Generals John J. Pershing, Douglas MacArthur, and Walter Krueger. After Pearl Harbor, General George C. Marshall made him commander of the Allied Forces landing in North Africa in November 1942; on D-Day, 1944, he was Supreme Commander of the troops invading France.

After World War II, Eisenhower became President of Columbia University, then took leave to assume supreme command over the new NATO forces being assembled in 1951. Republican emissaries to his headquarters near Paris persuaded him to run for President in 1952 and he won a sweeping victory.

He tried to reduce the strains of the Cold War. In 1953, the signing of a truce brought an armed peace along the border of South Korea. The death of Stalin the same year caused shifts in relations with Russia. New Russian leaders consented to a peace treaty neutralizing Austria. Meanwhile, both Russia and the United States had developed hydrogen bombs. With the threat of such destructive force hanging over the world, Eisenhower met with the leaders of the British, French, and Russian governments at Geneva in July 1955. Eisenhower proposed that the United States and Russia exchange blueprints of each other's military establishments and provide facilities for aerial photography to other countries. The Russians greeted the proposal with silence, but were so cordial throughout the meetings that tensions relaxed.

In September 1955, Eisenhower suffered a heart attack in Denver, Colorado. After seven weeks he left the hospital, and in February 1956 doctors reported his recovery. In November he was elected for his second term.

In domestic policy Eisenhower pursued a middle course, continuing most of the New Deal and Fair Deal programs, with a balanced budget a top priority. As desegregation of schools began, he sent troops into Little Rock, Arkansas, to assure compliance with the orders of a Federal court; he also ordered the complete desegregation of the Armed Forces. Eisenhower concentrated on maintaining world peace. Before he left office in January 1961, for his farm in Gettysburg, he urged the necessity of maintaining an adequate military strength, but cautioned that vast, long-continued military expenditures could breed potential dangers to our way of life. He concluded with a prayer for peace "in the goodness of time." Both themes remained timely and urgent when he died, after a long illness, on March 28, 1969 in Washington D.C.

Richard Nixon

Thirty-Seventh President
1969-1974

Born: January 9, 1913 in
Yorba Linda, California

Died: April 22, 1994 in
New York, New York

Married to
Patricia Ryan Nixon

Richard Milhous Nixon, America's 37th President, serving from 1969 to1974, was born January 9, 1913 in Yorba Linda, California.

Raised as an Evangelical Quaker by his mother, Hannah, who hoped he would become a Quaker missionary, his upbringing was marked by such conservative Evangelical Quaker observances as refraining from drinking, dancing, and swearing. His father was less religious, focusing on the family business, a store that sold groceries and gasoline. He attended Whittier College, a Quaker school, graduating second in his class, and Duke University Law School, where he received a full scholarship. He served as a noncombatant officer in the US Navy in World War II, and was a lawyer for PepsiCo. In 1940, he married Patricia Ryan; they had two daughters, Patricia (Tricia) and Julie. During World War II, Nixon served as a Navy lieutenant commander in the Pacific.

Upon leaving the service, he was elected to Congress from his California district. He was elected to the United

States House of Representatives from California in 1946, in a class of freshman war veterans that included his future rival John F. Kennedy, of Massachusetts. He was elected to the Senate in 1950, defeating actress/congress-woman Helen Gahagan, who Nixon accused during the campaign of having communist sympathies.

In 1952 General Eisenhower selected Nixon, age 39, to be his running mate. As Vice President, Nixon took on major duties in the Eisenhower Administration. Nominated for President by acclamation in 1960, he lost by a narrow margin to John F. Kennedy. He moved to New York City and worked as a lawyer. In the 1968 he defeated Hubert H. Humphrey and third-party candidate George C. Wallace to become the 37th U.S. President. His election in 1968 had climaxed a career unusual on two counts: his early success and his comeback after being defeated for President in 1960 and for Governor of California in 1962. In his 1972 bid for office, Nixon defeated Democratic candidate George McGovern by one of the widest margins on record.

Scandal broke within a few months, when his administration was embattled over the Watergate scandal, stemming from a break-in at the offices of the Democratic National Committee during the 1972 campaign. The break-in was traced to officials of the Committee to Re-elect the President. A number of administration officials resigned; some were later convicted of offenses connected with efforts to cover up the affair. Nixon denied any personal involvement, but the courts forced him to yield tape recordings which indicated that he had tried to divert the investigation. As a result of unrelated scandals in Maryland, Vice President Spiro T. Agnew resigned in 1973. Nixon nominated, and Congress approved, House Minority Leader Gerald R. Ford as Vice President. Faced with what seemed almost certain impeachment, Nixon announced on August 8, 1974, that he would resign the next day to begin "that process of healing which is so desperately needed in America." His successor Gerald R. Ford issued a pre-emptive pardon, ending the investigations.

Nixon's administration is credited with normalizing diplomatic relations with the People's Republic of China; the establishment of the Environmental Protection Agency; establishment of the Drug Enforcement Administration and the start of the space shuttle program.

In his last years Nixon succeeded in rehabilitating his public image, and gained respect as an elder statesman in the area of foreign affairs, being consulted by both Democratic and Republican successors to the Presidency. Nixon wrote many books after his departure from politics, including a history of the Vietnam war and his own personal memoirs.

Nixon died on April 22, 1994 in New York, New York at the age of 81, from complications related to a stroke, and was buried beside his wife Pat Nixon in the grounds of the Richard Nixon Presidential Library and Birthplace in Yorba Linda, California.

Gerald Ford

Thirty-Eighth President
1969-1974

Born: July 14, 1913 in Omaha,
Nebraska

Married to
Elizabeth Bloomer Ford

Gerald Rudolf Ford, Jr., the 38th President of the United States, served from 1974 to 1977, was born Leslie Lynch King, Jr., July 14, 1913 in Omaha, Nebraska. His biological father left his mother soon after his birth. His mother remarried, her husband adopted her son at which time he was renamed.

Ford attended public schools in Grand Rapids, graduating in the top five percent of his class. In 1931 he attended the University of Michigan where he was a B student, an outstanding football player, and was offered professional football contracts, which he declined because he wanted to go to law school. In 1935 he was hired to be an assistant football and head boxing coach at Yale University. In 1938 he began courses at Yale Law School while maintaining his position as coach. Ford graduated from law school in January 1941 and was admitted to the Michigan bar in June.

He served in the Navy from 1942 until 1946 mostly serving as the gunnery officer aboard the USS Monterey, a light aircraft carrier, which spent the bulk of the war in the South Pacific. During World War II he attained the rank of lieutenant commander in the Navy. After the war he returned to Grand Rapids, where he began the practice of law, and entered Republican politics. A few weeks before his election to Congress in 1948, he married Elizabeth Bloomer. They have four children: Michael, John, Steven, and Susan.

He remained a member of the House until he became Vice President in 1973. Ford had a consistent conservative record in the house. He was a supporter of the Marshall Plan and other anti-communist initiatives. He was a long-time friend of Richard Nixon, and supported him strongly within the party. He was a member of the Warren Commission that investigated the assassination of President Kennedy. In 1965 he became the House minority leader and opposed many of the Johnson domestic programs.

Ford was the first President to be appointed under the provisions of the 25th Amendment. President Nixon nominated him following the resignation of Vice President Agnew. He was confirmed in the Senate by 92-3 and in the House by 387-35. He took the oath of office on December 6, 1973. Ford became President eight months and three days later when Nixon resigned. President Ford's first major action in September 1974 was when he pardoned Nixon for all crimes that he may have committed during his Presidency. He felt that this was a way to put Watergate behind the nation. He also offered conditional amnesty to all the draft evaders and deserters from the Vietnam War. The draft evaders had to swear allegiance to the United States and do two years of community service. The deserters had to do two years of service in the branch of military from which they had deserted, but only a few evaders and deserters took up the offer.

Ford established his policies during his first year in office, and his first goal was to curb inflation and stimulate the economy. In foreign affairs Ford acted strongly to maintain U. S. power and prestige after the collapse of Cambodia and South Vietnam. Preventing a new war in the Middle East remained a top priority; by providing aid to both Israel and Egypt, his Administration helped persuade the two countries to accept an interim truce agreement. President Ford and Soviet leader Leonid I. Brezhnev set new limitations upon nuclear weapons.

President Ford won the Republican nomination for the Presidency in 1976, but lost the election to his Democratic opponent, former Georgia Governor Jimmy Carter. On his Inauguration Day, President Carter began his speech: "For myself and for our Nation, I want to thank my predecessor for all he has done to heal our land."

Ronald Reagan

Fortieth President
1981-1989

Born: February 6, 1911 in
Tampico, Illinois

Married to
Nancy Davis Reagan

Ronald Wilson Reagan, the 40th President of the United States, serving from 1981 to 1989, was born on February 6, 1911, in Tampico, Illinois, the second of two sons to John (Jack) Reagan and Nelle Wilson. In 1920 the family settled in Dixon, Illinois. In 1921, at age 11, Reagan was baptized in his mother's Disciples of Christ church in Dixon, and in 1924 he began attending Dixon's Northside High School.

In 1926, 15-year-old Reagan took a summer job as lifeguard in Lowell Park, two miles away from Dixon on the nearby Rock River where he worked for the next seven years, reportedly saving 77 people from drowning. In 1928, he entered Eureka College in Eureka, Illinois, graduating in 1932. He used imagination and his gift for storytelling and acting when he worked as a radio announcer. He was commissioned as a reserve cavalry officer in the U.S. Army in 1935. After Pearl Harbor he was activated and was assigned to the First Motion Picture Unit in the Army Air Corps, which made training and education films. He remained in Hollywood for the duration of the war and went on to have a successful Hollywood career as a leading man. His first screen credit was the starring role the 1937 movie Love is On the Air and by the end of 1939, he had appeared in 19 films. In 1940 he played the role of George "The Gipper" Gipp in the film Knute Rockne All American, from which he gained the nickname the Gipper, which he retained the rest of his life.

From his first marriage to actress Jane Wyman, he had two children, Maureen and Michael. Maureen died in 2001. In 1952 he married Nancy Davis, who was also an actress, and they had two children, Patricia Ann and Ronald Prescott.

Reagan began his political life as a liberal Democrat, supporting Franklin Delano Roosevelt. He gradually became a staunch social and fiscal conservative embarking upon the path that led him to a career in politics during his tenure as president of the Screen Actors Guild (SAG), where he became involved in disputes over the issue of Communism in the film industry. His political views shifted from liberal to conservative and he toured the country as a television host, becoming a spokesman for conservatism. In 1966 he was elected Governor of California by a margin of a million votes; he was re-elected in 1970. He won the Republican Presidential nomination in 1980 and chose former Texas Congressman and United Nations Ambassador George H. W. Bush as his running mate. On January 20, 1981, Reagan took office. On March 30, 1981, just 69 days into his presidency, he was shot by would-be assassin, John Hinckley, Jr., but quickly recovered and returned to duty.

Reagan is credited with increasing military spending, deploying U.S. Pershing II missiles in Germany in response to the Soviet stationing of missiles near Europe, pushing for the deployment of the Peacekeeper missile system, negotiating nuclear arms reduction treaties, proposing the Strategic Defense Initiative, increasing the federal deficit, greatly escalating the war on drugs, ending the high inflation that damaged the economy under his predecessors, Jimmy Carter and Gerald Ford, helping to win the Cold War, firing air traffic controllers when they illegally struck.

In 1992, four years after leaving office, Reagan was diagnosed with Alzheimer's disease and the disease began to slowly take over his brain and body, forcing him to live his post-presidency in quiet isolation.

On February 6, 1998, Washington National Airport in Washington, DC was renamed Ronald Reagan Washington National Airport. Also, the aircraft carrier USS Ronald Reagan (CVN-76) was christened on March 4, 2001, making it one of the very few United States Navy ships to be named after a living person. In 2004, Reagan turned 93, making him the oldest former president in American history.

George H.W. Bush

Forty-First President
1989-1993

Born: June 12, 1924 In
Milton, Massachusetts

Married to
Barbara Pierce Bush

George Herbert Walker Bush, the country's 41st President, serving from 1989 to 1993, was born June 12, 1924 in Milton, Massachusetts to Prescott Bush and Dorothy Walker. His father served as a Senator from Connecticut and was a partner in the leading investment banking firm Brown Brothers Harriman.

George Bush attended Phillips Academy in Andover, Massachusetts from 1936 to 1942, where he was captain of the baseball team, and was a member of an exclusive fraternity called the A.U.V, or "Auctoritas, Unitas, Veritas," which is Latin for "Authority, Unity, Truth". While attending Phillips Academy Bush learned of the surprise attack on Pearl Harbor, and after graduating in June 1942, he joined the US Navy. He was a naval aviator during World War II, the youngest ever at that time, and earned the Distinguished Flying Cross for his service in the Pacific Theater. After the War he attended Yale University, and was inducted into the secret society Skull and Bones, helping him to build friendships and political support.

Bush ventured into the Texas oil business after the war and secured a position with Dresser through his father's investment banking relationship with the company. He married Barbara Pierce on January 6, 1945. They had six children: George W., Pauline Robinson "Robin" who died of leukemia in 1953; John (Jeb); Neil; Marvin; and Dorothy Walker. The family has built on his and his father's political successes, with his son George W. Bush's Governorship of Texas and subsequent election as President, and his son Jeb Bush's election as Governor of Florida.

In 1964, he ventured into conventional politics by running against Democratic Senator Ralph Yarborough, but lost in the 1964 Democratic landslide. He was later elected in 1966 and 1968 to the House of Representatives from the 7th District of Texas. He lost his second attempt at a Senate seat in 1970. Bush briefly served in several positions throughout the 1970s, under Presidents Richard Nixon and Gerald Ford, including Chairman of the Republican National Committee, United States Ambassador to the United Nations, US Envoy to communist China, Director of the Central Intelligence Agency and board member of the Committee on the Present Danger.

In 1980, Bush ran for President, losing in the Republican Party primaries to Ronald Reagan. Reagan chose Bush as his Vice President, placing him on the winning Republican Presidential ticket of 1980. The Reagan/Bush ticket won again in 1984, against the Democratic ticket of Walter Mondale/Geraldine Ferraro. In 1988, after eight years as Vice President, Bush ran for President with Senator Dan Quayle as his running mate, defeating Michael Dukakis.

Bush faced a dramatically changing world, as the Cold War ended, the Communist empire dissolved, and the

Berlin Wall fell marking the end of the Soviet Union and the resignation of President Mikhail Gorbachev. In other areas of foreign policy, President Bush sent American troops into Panama to overthrow the corrupt regime of General Manuel Noriega, who was threatening the security of the canal and the Americans living there. Noriega was brought to the United States for trial as a drug trafficker. When Iraqi President Saddam Hussein invaded Kuwait and threatened to move into Saudi Arabia, Bush rallied the United Nations, the U. S. people, and Congress and sent 425,000 American troops to Kuwait. They were joined by 118,000 troops from allied nations in the 100-hour land battle dubbed Desert Storm defeating Iraq's million-man army.

Bush was defeated by Bill Clinton in the 1992 election and retired from public life.

George W. Bush

Forty-Third President
2001-

Born: July 6, 1946 in
New Haven, Connecticut

Married to
Laura Welch Bush

George Walker Bush, the 43rd President of the United States took office in 2001 and at press time is running for re-election against Massachusetts Senator John Kerry. He was born July 6, 1946 in New Haven, Connecticut to George and Barbara Bush. He grew up in Midland and Houston, Texas and like his father, was educated at Phillips Academy (Andover) (September 1961 - June 1964) and Yale University (September 1964 - May 1968). While at Yale he joined Delta Kappa Epsilon where he was president from October 1965 until graduation, and the Skull and Bones Society. He played baseball during his freshman year and rugby during his junior and senior years. He received a bachelor's degree in history in 1968.

Immediately after graduating from Yale, Bush joined the Texas Air National Guard. In 1970, he became an F-102 pilot and was promoted to first lieutenant. In 1972 he was granted a transfer to Alabama where he worked as political director in the Senate campaign of Winton M. Blount. In September 1973 he was granted permission to end his six-year commitment six months early to attend Harvard and transferred to inactive reserve status shortly before being honorably discharged on October 1, 1973. He entered Harvard Business School in 1973 where he earned a Master of Business Administration (MBA) in 1975, making him the first U.S. President to hold an MBA degree.

Bush married Laura Welch in 1977. In 1978 he ran unsuccessfully for the House of Representatives. In 1986, at age 40, he became a born-again Christian, converting from Episcopalian to his wife's denomination, Methodism. They have twin daughters, Barbara and Jenna, born in 1981. Barbara is currently a student at Yale University and Jenna attends the University of Texas at Austin.

Bush is the second person to become U.S. President whose father was also President. John Adams, the second President, and John Quincy Adams, the sixth, were father and son; Bush's father, George H. W. Bush, was the 41st President of the United States.

Bush began his career in the oil industry in 1979 when he began operations of Arbusto Energy, an oil and gas exploration company he formed in 1977. The oil crisis of the late 1970s hurt the company and, after a name change to Bush Exploration Co., he sold the company in 1984 to Spectrum 7, another Texas oil and gas exploration firm. Under the terms of the sale, Bush became CEO of Spectrum 7. The oil crisis of 1985-1986 bankrupted Spectrum 7 which was saved by a buyout from Harken Energy Corp in 1986 with Bush becoming a director of Harken.

He was elected Governor of Texas on November 8, 1994 and in 1998 became the first Texas governor to be elected for two consecutive four-year terms. Bush campaigned on such issues as allowing religious charities to compete on an equal basis for participation in federally funded programs; and supporting tax cuts, the use of school vouchers, drilling for oil in the Arctic National Wildlife Refuge; and redesigning the US military.

Bush became President on January 20, 2001, winning one of the closest general elections in American history, defeating Democratic Vice President Al Gore by only five electoral votes, and winning in 30 of the 50 states; while Gore won the nationwide popular vote. It was the third consecutive presidential election in which no candidate received a majority of the popular vote. It was the first presidential election since the 1888 election in which a candidate lost the popular vote while winning the electoral college vote. The outcome was decided by only a few hundred popular votes in Florida, where Bush's brother Jeb was governor. After a U.S. Supreme Court decision in mid-December, Gore decided to end legal actions about the elections. Among Bush's most important legislation were several tax cuts, the No Child Left Behind Act, and the Medicare reforms. Of the $2.4 trillion budget for 2005 about $450 billion are planned to be spent on defense. Congress approved $87 billion for Iraq and Afghanistan in November, and had approved an earlier $79 billion package last spring. Most of those funds were for U.S. military operations in the two countries. No Child Left Behind targets supporting early learning, measures student performance, gives options over failing schools, and ensures more resources for schools.

Republican National Conventions

1856: Philadelphia, Pa.	1932: Chicago, Ill.
1860: Chicago, Ill.	1936: Cleveland, Ohio
1864: Baltimore, Md.	1940: Philadelphia, Pa.
1868: Chicago, Ill.	1944: Chicago, Ill.
1872: Philadelphia, Pa.	1948: Philadelphia, Pa.
1876: Cincinnati, Ohio	1952: Chicago, Ill.
1880: Chicago, Ill.	1956: San Francisco, Calif.
1884: Chicago, Ill.	1960: Chicago, Ill.
1888: Chicago, Ill.	1964: San Francisco, Calif.
1892: Minneapolis, Minn.	1968: Miami Beach, Fla.
1896: St. Louis, Mo.	1972: Miami Beach, Fla.
1900: Philadelphia, Pa.	1976: Kansas City, Mo.
1904: Chicago, Ill.	1980: Detroit, Mich.
1908: Chicago, Ill.	1984: Dallas, Tex.
1912: Chicago, Ill.	1988: New Orleans, La.
1916: Chicago, Ill.	1992: Houston, Tex.
1920: Chicago, Ill.	1996: San Diego, Calif.
1924: Cleveland, Ohio	2000: Philadelphia, Pa.
1928: Kansas City, Mo.	2004: New York, NY

Republican Organizations

(in alphabetical order)

African American Republican Leadership Council (AARLC)
The Ronald Reagan Building
1300 Pennsylvania Avenue, NW
Suite 700
Washington, DC 20005
Phone: 202-675-8338
Fax: 202-546-6589
http://www.aarlc.org

The mission and purpose of the African American Republican Leadership Council (AARLC) is to break the liberal democrat stranglehold over Black America.

Bull Moose Republicans
1747 Pennsylvania Avenue #157
Washington DC 20006
info@bullmooserepublicans.com

Founded in the spirit of Teddy Roosevelt, Bull Moose Republicans is an organization committed to resurrecting the Republican Party's dedication to the inclusive and reform values of Abraham Lincoln and Teddy Roosevelt.

Christian Coalition of America

The Christian Coalition was founded in 1989 by Pat Robertson to give Christians a voice in government. They represent a growing group of over 2 million people of faith to have a voice in the conversation we call democracy.

Driven by the belief that people of faith have a right and a responsibility to be involved in the world around them, the Christian Coalition is dedicated to equipping and educating God's people with the resources and information to battle against anti-family legislation. Whether on a stump, in print, or over the airways that involvement includes community, social and political action.

Since the beginning, the Christian Coalition has provided critical pro-family information in order to challenge individuals, churches and community groups to make a difference at all levels of government. Effective citizen activism begins with knowledge, and the Christian Coalition's ability to break down the complexity of politics and convey those issues clearly with solvable opportunities is what makes their information different.

Goals include:

- Strengthening the family.
- Protecting innocent human life.
- Returning education to local and parental control.
- Easing the tax burden on families.
- Punishing criminals and defending victims' rights.
- Protecting young people and our communities from the pollution of pornography.
- Defending the institution of marriage.
- Protecting religious freedom.
  Five - Fold Mission
- Represent the pro-family point of view before local councils, school boards, state legislatures and Congress.

- Speak out in the public arena and in the media.
- Train leaders for effective social and political action.
- Inform pro-family voters about timely issues and legislation.
- Protest anti-Christianity bigotry and defend the rights of people of faith.

Club for Growth
Club for Growth and Club for Growth PAC
1776 K Street, NW, Suite 300
Washington, DC 20006
Phone: 202-955-5500
College Republican National Committee

600 Pennsylvania Ave SE
Suite 215
Washington, DC 20003
Phone: (888) 765-3564
Fax: (202) 608-1429
Email: info@crnc.org

The College Republican National Committee is the nationwide coordinating organization for the Republican youth movement. With over 120,000 members on 1,148 college campuses, the College Republican National Committee plays an integral role in the election of Republican candidates as well as the communication of a conservative message to college students. The CRNC has tripled in size in recent years.

The Council of Republicans for Environmental Advocacy
2117 L Street NW #303
Washington, DC 20037
Phone: 202-625-7110

Republicans who believe conservation benefits all Americans. The Council of Republican for Environmental Advocacy, (CREA) is committed to preserving America's natural resources, air, water, and scenic beauty for future generations. CREA's mission is to foster environmental protection by promoting fair, community-based solutions to environmental challenges, highlighting Republican environmental accomplishments and building on our Republican tradition of conservation. CREA believes that environmental goals are reached by finding common ground between individuals, the private sector and local conservationists...results that would be impossible to achieve without cooperation.

Log Cabin Republicans

Washington, D.C. Headquarters
1607 17th St N.W.
Washington, DC 20009
Phone: (202) 347-5306
Fax: (202) 347-5224
communications@logcabin.org

Log Cabin is over 25 years old. The organization started in California-created to battle the nation's first anti-gay ballot measure. Aside from working within the party for change, Log Cabin continues building new alliances in the gay and lesbian community. Both parties have an important role to play in advancing civil rights. Log Cabin's position is that without allies in the Republican Party, the push for equality will take decades longer.

Mainstream Republicans of Washington
7620 W. 21st Ave.
Kennewick WA 99338-9163

6920 West 21st Place
Richland, WA 99338
http://www.washingtonmainstream.org/

Mainstream exists to help nominate Republican candidates who can win the general elections.

National Association of Urban Republican
County Chairman
2089 German Church Road
Indianapolis IN 46239
Phone: 317-894-7592
Fax: 312-891-1906

National Conference of Republican County Officials
310 First Street, SE
Washington DC 20003
Phone: 202-863-8600
Fax: 202-863-8657

National Federation of Grand Order of Pachyderm Clubs
511 Central Avenue, #3
Great Falls MT 59401
Phone: 888-467-2249
Fax: 406-771-3941

The National Federation of the Grand Order of Pachyderm Clubs, Inc. is an officially recognized allied organization of the Republican Party. Patterned after civic clubs, Pachyderm Clubs offer programs centered around politics and government. Pachyderm Clubs can be the continuity for the Republican Party from election to election in that unlike the party structure, Pachyderm Clubs remain active all year.

Pachyderm Clubs do not endorse issues nor candidates in contested primary elections. This prohibition provides a neutral forum for the discussion of divisive issues within the Republican Party. In many communities, the Pachyderm Club has become a healing influence within the party and a subtle reminder that Republicans agree on a much larger number of issues than we disagree on.

The Pachyderm Club movement is one of the most practical means by which broad citizen participation in politics may be achieved.

Over 60 Pachyderm Clubs are located in 16 states around the U.S. and are growing every day.

National Federation of Republican Assemblies (NFRA)

The NFRA is an outgrowth of the California Republican Assembly and is our nation's oldest and largest Republican volunteer organization. The NFRA is the national umbrella organization for all of the nationwide state Republican Assembly organizations.

The NFRA is dedicated to working within the Republican Party to promote the active participation of our members toward the endorsement, support, and election, of principled conservative Republican candidates.

"Through unity there is strength...A well organized group of like minded individuals can bring responsible citizens to public office in every level of government." - Abraham Lincoln

National Federation of Republican Women

The National Federation of Republican Women is one of the largest and most influential women's political organizations in the country.

Founded in 1938, the Federation is a grassroots organization with 100,000 members and 1,800 local units nationwide. Members come together as a collective force to advance the power of women through political access and participation. Its mission is to help women from all walks of life become players at the political table nationally, statewide and locally, and to strengthen the Republican Party by recruiting, training and electing candidates; advocating the Party's philosophy and initiatives; and, empowering women of all ages, ethnicities and backgrounds in the political process.

National Republican Congressional Committee (NRCC)
320 First Street, S.E.
Washington, D.C. 20003
Phone: (202) 479-7000
http://nrcc.org

National Republican Heritage Groups Council
5825 3rd Place, NW
Washington DC 20011
Phone: 708-423-8206
Fax: 708-423-6924

National Republican Legislators Association (NRLA)
6348 Crosswoods Drive
Falls Church, VA 22044
Phone: (703) 333-5102
Fax: (703) 333-5103

The National Republican Legislators Association (NRLA) is the official organization and political committee of the nation's Republican state legislators. Its membership consists of Republican state legislators and legislators-elect of the United States and its territories.

As provided in the NRLA Bylaws, its purposes are as follows:

To assist in the election of Republican state legislators through direct candidate assistance and other means;

To maximize Republican control of state legislative chambers;

To promote smaller and less intrusive government, lower taxes, volunteerism, and a return of power to the states consistent with the Tenth Amendment to the U.S. Constitution;

To promote the integrity of the several legislatures as equal coordinate branches of government at the state and national level;

To advance the knowledge and effectiveness of individual Republican state legislators and candidates through education and coordination activities;

To facilitate communications and cooperation among its members and the White House, the Republican National Committee, Republican State Committees, Republicans in Congress, National Conference of State Legislatures, American Legislative Exchange Council, Council of State Governments, and other organizations;

To enable Republican state legislators to take their proper position in expressing the philosophy of the Republican party within the national party framework;

To assist in the solution of significant national public policy problems and in related lobbying efforts; and

To honor the innovations and outstanding accomplishments of Republican state legislators.

The mission of the NRLA during the 2002-03 period is to: (1) raise funds to underwrite the provision of direct candidate assistance, the maintenance of a Washington, DC office, the conduct of outreach activities, the publication of a quarterly newsletter, the operation of a web site, the training of Republican legislators and candidates, and other activities; and (2) implement NRLA activities as funds become available.

National Republican Senatorial Committee (NRSC)
It is the sole responsibility of the NRSC to make sure that Republican Senate candidates are elected to the United States Senate.

NRSC
Ronald Reagan Republican Center
425 2nd Street, NE
Washington, DC 20002
Phone: 202-675-6000
websitecomments@nrsc.org

Member Programs:

NRSC E-Members

An NRSC E-Membership, the first step towards helping Republicans push President Bush's Agenda through the Senate, is free and available to anyone with access to the Internet. E-Membership provides a free subscription to weekly e-newsletter The Chairman's Report.

NRSC Platinum E-Members

Platinum E-Membership is the premier online NRSC donor group. Platinum E-members receive a more comprehensive, weekly email update on U.S. Senate races. A $50 annual gift is required for membership.

Republican Presidential Task Force

The Republican Presidential Task Force was founded by President Reagan in 1981 with one focus: to permanently advance his work towards building a "freer, stronger America."

Republican Senatorial Inner Circle

Founded in 1979 and brought to the forefront of the American political landscape by President Ronald Reagan, the Inner Circle has been and continues to be a major force in the Republican Party. Its mission is to protect and expand on the narrow Republican Senate Majority by re-electing incumbent Senators, electing new Republican Senators, and making sure President George W. Bush is re-elected.

Republican Presidential Roundtable

Early in 1987, faced with a newly-elected Democrat-controlled Senate, President Ronald Reagan founded the Republican Presidential Roundtable. He sought not only to restore a Republican Senate Majority but to create a unique forum in American politics which would bring together 400 of this nation's most prominent business and civic leaders. President Reagan wanted to enlist their greater involvement in the party and country.

Republican Senate Council

The Republican Senate Council provides the forum for top leaders in business and Washington representatives to share with Republican Senators their frustrations over government regulation and help seek new ways to promote economic growth.

Republican Senatorial Trust

First organized in 1977, the Senatorial Trust has remained determined to shape a positive destiny for our nation. Republican Senators meet with the Senatorial Trust four times a year. These meetings help foster future political and legislative victories and enable Trust members to share innovative ideas based on their real world experience. The support of the Trust will be crucial to advancing President Bush's tax cuts, education and Social Security initiatives, and other long overdue reforms, through a very divided Congress.

Republicans Abroad International
209 Pennsylvania Avenue, SE
Washington DC 20003
Phone: 202-608-1423
Fax: 202-608-1431
http://www.republicansabroad.org

Republicans Abroad is the International Arm of the GOP and was formed to enlist the personal energy and leadership of Republicans living overseas. In fact, more than six million Americans live abroad, a number larger than the populations of 24 states in the Union. Republicans Abroad helps the Republican Party develop policy and campaign strategy at the highest levels. Financial contributions to Republicans Abroad are critically important to the GOP's ongoing party building, campaign, and candidate support activities.

Republicans for Environmental Protection (REP)
3200 Carlisle Blvd., #228
Albuquerque, NM 87110
Phone: 505-889-4544
info@repamerica.org
www.repamerica.org or www.rep.org

REP America was formed in 1995 to resurrect the GOP's great conservation tradition and to restore natural resource conservation and sound environmental protection as fundamental elements of the Republican Party's vision for America.

Republican Attorneys General Association
310 First St. SE
Washington DC 20003
Phone: 202-863-8673
Fax: 202-842-4447

Republican Governors Association
555 11th Street, NW, Suite 700
Washington, D.C. 20004
Phone: (202) 662-4140
Fax: (202) 662-4924
www.rga.org

Founded in 1963, the Republican Governors Association (RGA), is the official public policy and political organization of the Republican Governors of the United States. The RGA maintains a leadership role at the forefront of national policy-making. Meeting with congressional leaders regularly, Republican Governors remain actively engaged in setting the agenda in areas such as tax cuts, welfare and education reform. In addition to influencing the national agenda, the RGA assists in the election of Republican gubernatorial candidates and the re-election of incumbant governors.

The RGA mission is:

1. To assist in the election of Republican gubernatorial candidates and the re-election of incumbent Republican Governors.

2. To utilize the talent, knowledge, creativity of the governors to effectively debate and shape public policy on issues affecting the states; and

3. To enable Republican Governors to express, develop and promote the philosophy of the Republican party at the state and local levels nationwide.

Republican Jewish Coalition
50 F Street, NW, Suite 100
Washington, DC 20001
Phone: 202-638-6688
Fax: 202-638-6694
rjc@rjchq.org

Republican Leadership Council (RLC)
3222 M Street, NW
Suite U 501
Washington, DC 20007
Phone: 202-547-1700
Fax: 1-800-619-5265

The Republican Leadership Council was formed in 1997 by leading Republicans throughout the country concerned that the Republican Party is being increasingly defined by the actions of an intolerant vocal minority that divides the GOP. The RLC is dedicated to building a stronger Republican majority by promoting the fundamental conservative ideals of lower taxes, less government and more personal freedom.

Republican Liberty Caucus
44 Summerfield Street
Thousand Oaks, California 91360
Toll-Free: (866) RLC-Liberty [752-5423]

The Republican Liberty Caucus (RLC) is a grassroots, nationwide organization affiliated with the Republican Party (GOP). The goal of the RLC is to elect pro-liberty individuals to office.

The RLC was founded in 1990, and now has members in every state.

Republican Main Street Partnership
1350 I Street, NW
Suite 560
Washington, DC 20005
Phone: 202-682-3143
Fax: 202-682-3943
E-Mail: republicanmainst@mindspring.com

The Republican Main Street Partnership was founded in 1998 to promote thoughtful leadership in the Republican Party, to serve as a voice for centrist Republicans and to partner with individuals, organizations and institutions that share centrist values.The Partnership pursues public policies that reflect a limited, but responsible role for government and that are designed to achieve fiscal responsibility, economic growth, improvements in the human condition and a nation that is globally competitive and secure. Partnership members include individuals who are interested in moderate Republican policies, focusing on governance and on finding common sense solutions to national problems."The Republican Main Street Partnership is an organization of party members and public officials committed to building America's principled but pragmatic center within the Republican Party and throughout the nation. The Partnership contributes to the nation's governance through developing and promoting creative public policies for implementation at appropriate levels of government."

Republican Mayors and Local Officials
400 North Capitol Street, NW, Suite 585
Washington DC 20001
Phone: 202-783-2704
Fax: 202-393-7718

Republican National Coalition for Life
RNC/Life PAC
P.O. Box 618
Alton, IL 62002

COLLEEN PARRO, Executive Director
5009 Harvest Hill Road
Dallas, TX 75244
Phone: 972-387-4160
FAX 972-387-3830
http://www.rnclife.org

The Republican National Coalition for Life PAC supports Republican congressional candidates who are unconditionally pro-life. Candidates who recognize the inherent right to life of every innocent human being, from conception until natural death, without discrimination, are eligible for support by RNC/Life PAC.

Republican National Committee (RNC)
310 First Street, SE
Washington, DC 20003
Phone: 202-863-8500
Fax: 202-863-8820
Email: info@gop.com

The Republican Party was born in the early 1850s by anti-slavery activists and individuals who believed that government should grant western lands to settlers free of charge.

Republican National Hispanic Assembly
P.O. Box 1882
Washington, DC 20013-1882
Washington DC 20013-1882
Phone: 202-544-6700
Fax: 202-544-6869
http://www.rnha.org

The RNHA grew out of the Hispanic Finance Committee. The Finance Committee raised over a quarter of a million dollars in nine states. Its goal was to build an organization to foster the principles of the Republican Party in the Hispanic Community, to provide Hispanic Americans with a forum to play an influential role in local, state and national party activities, and to increase the number of Republican Hispanic elected officials. The fall campaign of 1972 saw the first group of RNHA members and officials in action. They were discussing issues, and helping to get out the Hispanic vote. In 1974 the RNHA was officially organized by a group of Hispanic Republicans under the leadership of then-incumbent RNC Chairman George Bush. Since that time, RNHA has been the only Hispanic Republican organization recognized as an allied of the Republican National Committee (RNC).

Republican National Lawyers Assn. (RNLA)
PO Box 18965
Washington, DC   20036
Phone: 703-719-6335
Fax: 703-719-6335
thielen@republicanlawyer.net

As the principal national organization of Republican lawyers, the Association has a targeted set of missions, all complementary, and none of which duplicate missions accomplished elsewhere. Each member of the Association and every local chapter must ascribe to the accomplishment of these missions, which include: Advancing Professionalism, Advancing Election Integrity, Advancing Career Opportunity, Advancing Republican Ideals.

Republican Pro-Choice Coalition
The Fairchild Building
499 South Capitol Street, SW Suite 414
Washington, DC 20003
Toll Free: 1-877-GOP-CHOICE (467-2464)
Phone: 202-484-3040
Fax: 202-484-3041
http://www.rpcc.org

The Republican Pro-Choice Coalition is an organization of Republican men and women throughout the United States, who believe in the party's traditional principles of individual liberty, strong national security and sound economic reason. They endorse the 'big tent' philosophy of inclusion and tolerance on social issues.

Republican Research Council
P.O. Box 151
Kensington, MD 20895
Phone: 301-554-0554
E-Mail: republicanresearchcouncil@erols.com

The Republican Research Council is a nonprofit organization that helps Republican candidates and their campaigns by researching what works and what doesn't work in a political campaign.

Republican Youth Majority
101 D St.
Washington, DC 20003
Phone: 202-546-1300
Fax: 202-546-7212
info@rym.org

The Republican Youth Majority is a nationwide network of students and young professionals who believe in developing an inclusive generation of pro-choice, pro-environment, and fiscally conservative Republican leaders to ensure a long-term Republican majority well into the 21st Century.

Ronald Reagan Presidential Foundation
40 Presidential Drive, Simi Valley, CA 93065
Phone: 805-522-2977
Fax: 805-520-9702
http://www.reaganfoundation.org

The Ronald Reagan Presidential Foundation is a non-profit organization located in Simi Valley, California that sustains: The Ronald Reagan Presidential Library and Museum; The Center for Public Affairs; and The Presidential Learning Center. The mission of the Ronald Reagan Presidential Foundation is to complete President Reagan's unfinished work and to promote the timeless principles he championed of Individual Liberty, Economic Opportunity, Global Democracy, and National Pride.

Ripon Society
1300 L Street, NW
Suite 900
Washington, DC 20005
info@riponsoc.org

The Ripon Society, founded in 1962, is a nonprofit research, public policy, and social welfare organization. It furthers fiscal prudence; social diversity and inclusion; limited and responsible government; and a pragmatic, long-term foreign policy that recognizes the nation's international responsibilities and a strong national defense.

Susan B. Anthony List
1800 Diagonal Rd.
Suite 285
Alexandria, Virginia 22314
Phone: 703-683-5558
info@sba-list.org

The Susan B. Anthony List is a 501 (c)(4) not-for-profit membership organization with a connected political action committee (SBA List Candidate Fund) whose mission is to end abortion in the United States and to get more women active in the political and legislative arena.

Teenage Republicans (TARs)
10620-C Crestwood Drive
Manassas, VA 20109
Mailing Address:
PO Box 1896
Manassas, VA 20108-1896
Phone: 703-368-4214
Fax: 703-368-0830

TARS@TeenAgeRepublicans.org
Young Republican National Federation, Inc.
600 Pennsylvania Avenue, SE Suite 302
Washington DC 20003
Phone: 202-608-1417
Fax: 202-608-1430

A Glossary of Terms

Beauty contest — A preliminary vote usually taken early in the electoral process within a party; it expresses a non-binding preference for one or another of the party's candidates. This preference is not linked to the selection of convention delegates.

Caucus — Literally, it means "a meeting," and it is one of the main mechanisms used by modern American political parties to nominate their candidate for president. In the presidential nomination process, it now denotes a meeting of local party activists at the precinct level who select, in an open forum, delegates to county meetings. These delegates in turn select delegates to state meetings; and these state-level conventions select delegates to the party's national convention. The purpose of this layered caucus system is to open political participation to as many people as possible, and to provide greater incentives to recruitment of fresh talent into party politics than merely voting in a primary election. From February to June of a presidential election year, the major political parties of every state conduct either caucuses or primary elections ("primaries"). By tradition, the rural, midwestern state of Iowa has the first set of caucuses in the nation (even before the first primary in New Hampshire), and so it has a big impact on the race, even though it is a small state with so few delegates.

Conservative — In American politics, someone who is right-of-center politically. Of the two major parties, the Republicans are generally considered more conservative. In the United States, conservatives usually emphasize free-market economic principles and often prefer state and local governmental power to federal power. Traditionally, conservative support has come from business leaders. Candidates and voters commonly refer to themselves and others as conservative, moderate or liberal.

Convention — A meeting, at state or national level, of "delegates" from a political party. These delegates vote for the person they want their party to nominate for political office. The nominated candidate will then compete in the general election with the candidates of other parties, and against any independent candidates, not endorsed by a political party. In modern U.S. presidential politics, "convention" usually refers to the national conventions of the Democratic and Republican parties, held every four years, during the Summer before the general election (which is held in November). These conventions, which include delegates from all states of the Union, the District of Columbia, and U.S. territories, formally nominate the presidential candidate.

Delegate — An official representative selected by members of his or her party to a national or state political convention.

Democratic Party — One of the two current major political parties. For the most part, particularly since the early 1930s, the Democrats have been considered the party of less affluent people, and have supported an activist role for the federal government in the economic and social sectors. The first Democratic president, Andrew Jackson, was elected in 1828, as the seventh U.S. president. The Democratic party is generally considered to be more liberal or less conservative than the other current major party: the Republican Party.

Electoral base — A politician's "electoral base" is considered to be the heart of his or her constituency, i.e., the groups of people who will usually vote for him or her whatever the prevailing political conditions at any given time, often out of party loyalty (contrast with swing voters), or some other combination of variables such as ethnicity, gender, religion, ideology, military service, geography, or positions on issues. In other countries, "electoral base" is often called the "vote bank."

Electoral College — The electoral college is the group of electors, chosen by voters throughout the U.S. on a state basis, on election day, who then meet and formally select the next president of the United States. The selection is by a majority of 270 votes out of the 538 electors. The electoral college system is mandated by the U.S. Constitution.

Get-Out-the-Vote ("GOTV") Operations — In the last few days of a campaign, particularly on election day, campaigns usually focus most of their resources on getting their electoral base out to the polls to vote. Such operations (abbreviated as "GOTV" by campaign managers) include television and radio broadcast appeals, telephone banks of volunteers and campaign workers who call voters' homes, reminding them to vote, "soundtrucks" with amplified speakers that drive through neighborhoods of likely supporters, volunteer drivers who drive likely supporters (particularly the elderly or disabled) to the polls, and dissemination of campaign paraphernalia (such as buttons, balloons, brochures, flyers, banners, lawn signs, posters).

GOP — An abbreviation for "Grand Old Party" — nickname of the Republican Party.

Independent — In U.S. politics, this term denotes a voter, who, when registering to vote, does not declare affiliation with the Republicans, Democrats, or other political parties or does not consider himself or herself to be a member of a political party. Likewise, the term can also refer to a candidate for office who is running on the basis of personal identity rather than party affiliation.

Liberal — In American politics, "liberals" tend to be people who are somewhat ideologically left-of-center. They tend to favor more power at the federal level and federal intervention to regulate economic issues and certain social issues, particularly social issues involving civil liberties, and the rights of minority groups. Of the two major parties, the Democrats are generally considered more liberal. Traditionally, the bases of liberal support have been among minorities, urban voters, labor unions and academics, though that is evolving as U.S. politics change. Candidates and voters commonly refer to themselves and others as conservative, moderate or liberal.

Midterm elections — This term refers to elections held in-between presidential elections, that is, two years after the previous, and two years before the next, presidential elections. Each midterm election selects one-third of the 100 members of the U.S. Senate and all 435 members of the House of Representatives, as well as many state and local officials.

Persuasion activities — Campaigns frame or define a message that will appeal to the undecided voters, and convey that message through advertising (television, radio, and print), direct-mail to the voters' homes, door-to-door and street-corner campaigning by volunteers or campaign workers, personal appearances and speeches by the candidate, candidate appearances at debates, endorsements and testimonials, and favorable coverage in the news (referred to as "free media" because candidates did not have to buy advertising space or time. Campaigns generally do not waste resources attempting to persuade voters that comprise the opposition's electoral base. As for their own electoral base, campaigns generally target get-out-the-vote resources.

Platform — A formal statement of position on major political issues drafted by a candidate or a political party. In other countries, the "platform" may be called the party "manifesto." The major parties ratify their platforms at their national conventions.

Plurality — A plurality of votes is a total vote received by a candidate greater than that received by any opponent but less than a 50 percent majority of the vote. In other words, if one candidate receives 30 percent of the vote, another candidate receives 30 percent of the vote, and a third candidate receives 40 percent, that third candidate has a plurality of the votes, and wins the election. Abraham Lincoln and Bill Clinton are examples of presidents who received a majority of the electoral vote, but only a plurality of the popular vote in a competitive three-way election contest.

Primary — A "closed" primary is a system of selecting a party's candidate for office in an intraparty election in which only registered members of that party may vote. Most state primaries are closed. An "open" primary is a system of selecting a party's candidate for office in which voters registered with other parties and "independent" voters (i.e., unaffiliated with any party) may also vote. This kind of primary is also known as a "cross-over" primary. The major political parties in every state choose delegates for their party's national nominating conventions, by means of either a primary or a caucus. By tradition, the state of New Hampshire has the first primary (soon after the Iowa caucuses), and so it has big impact on setting the stage for the rest of the race, even though it is a small state with so few delegates.

Reagan Democrats — Democrats who voted for Ronald Reagan for president during the 1980s. It has become a generic term for swing voters in the Democratic party.

Realignment — In U.S. politics, this term refers to occasional historic shifts of public opinion and voter concerns that either undermine or enhance one or another party's traditional base of support. The term is generally applied to national elections which clearly shift the majority and minority status of the two U.S. major political parties, or which replace one of the two major political parties with one that previously had been a "third party." Realignment may be based on many factors, such as the reaction to party positions on a critical issue of national concern (as was the case with the slavery issue in the 1860s), credit or blame for handling a national crisis (such as the Great Depression of 1929) or substantial changes in the demographic make-up of the voting populace.

Republican Party ("GOP") — One of the two major U.S. political parties. During the 20th century, the Republican party has generally been the party of more affluent and conservative voters, and has favored economic and social policies that are somewhat less re-distributive than Democratic party policies. The first Republican president was Abraham Lincoln, the 16th U.S. president, elected in 1860. The Republicans emerged in a major party realignment, replacing the now defunct Whig Party as a major U.S. party. The nickname, often used in newspaper headlines or when a commentator wishes to abbreviate, is "GOP" (pronounced gee-oh-pee, not gop) which stands for a now antiquated and little-used term, "grand old party."

RINO — Republicans In Name Only

Straw poll — In modern presidential politics, a non-binding vote, often taken among party activists and usually at a very early stage in a candidate-selection process, to indicate which candidate or candidates are preferred by a local group.

Stump speech — The standard speech of a candidate for office, the one he or she is most likely to use, perhaps with slight variations, on normal occasions.

Super Tuesday — Primary elections are often held on Tuesdays, and Super Tuesdays are when primaries and caucuses are held in several states on the same day, with many delegates "up for grabs." If a candidate does particularly well on Super Tuesday, he or she will not only gain many delegates, but also press coverage and momentum. Since Super Tuesdays are seen as big events on the election calendar, they often have a large impact on the perception of where candidates stand in the race, causing front runners to solidify the perception of their invincibility, or lose ground to other candidates that do better than expected. Often, candidates that have were lagging in the opinion polls, and that failed to do well in the earlier primaries and caucuses, drop out of the race if they fail to do well on Super Tuesday (they also may find it difficult to raise additional campaign funds, because they are portrayed as not having a chance to win the nomination). Therefore, Super Tuesday may serve as the coup de grace on candidates' campaigns that were already in trouble after disappointing showings in the earlier caucuses and primaries, such as Iowa and New Hampshire.

Swing Voters, Ticket Splitters, and Persuadables — "Swing voters" are those that are not always loyal to a particular political party, and therefore are not part of any party's electoral base. They get their name because they might "swing" from one party to the other in different elections. "Ticket Splitters" is another name for swing voters, because many of them will vote for candidates from opposing parties for different offices on the same ballot (e.g., might vote Democratic for President and Republican for Senator, or vice versa). They get their name because they do not necessarily vote for all candidates on the same "ticket" or slate, thus these voters "split" their votes. When swing voters are undecided as to which candidate they will support, they are called "undecideds." Political campaign managers also refer to undecideds as "persuadables," because campaigns concentrate on persuading them, through various persuasion activities, to vote for their candidate. Campaigns generally consider the opposition's "natural" electoral base as unpersuadable, and consider their own "natural" electoral base as already likely to favor their own candidate. Thus, they do not waste resources on the former, and only "target" the latter for motivation or assistance to vote(called get-out-the-vote operations) on election day. Although swing voters are sometimes referred to as independents, they may be registered members of any political party. For example, Reagan Democrats is the term used for those Democratic voters who voted for the Republican president, Ronald Reagan in the 1980s. Reagan Democrats is often used today as a generic term for swing voters in the Democratic party.

Third party — In the parlance of American politics, "third party" refers to political parties outside the two-party system which are perceived to have a significant base of support. In the 20th century, that has come to mean a party that is not the Republican Party or the Democratic Party and can play some role in influencing the outcome of an election.

Resources

Republican National Committee
310 First Street, SE
Washington, DC 20003
Phone: 202-863-8500
Fax: 202-863-8820
E-mail: info@gop.com

PageWise, Inc.
815-A Brazos Street
PMB 534
Austin, TX 78701

Democratic National Committee
430 S. Capitol St. SE
Washington, DC 20003
Phone: 202-863-8000

The White House
1600 Pennsylvania Avenue NW
Washington, DC 20500
Comments: 202-456-1111
Switchboard: 202-456-1414
Fax: 202-456-2461
http://www.whitehouse.gov

Bibliography

William Safire, New Language of Politics, Revised Edition,
    Collier Books, New York, 1972

Ron Gunzburger

National Republican Congressional Committee

Republican National Committee

Democratic National Committee

Ulysses S. Grant Network Website

Campaigning with Grant, by Horace Porter

The Personal Memoirs of Ulysses S. Grant

The Personal Memoirs of Julia Dent Grant

Captain Sam Grant, by Lloyd Lewis

A Personal History of Ulysses S. Grant,
    by Albert D. Richardson

StarGroup International Book Division

For many years StarGroup International has produced books for clients to use as a media or marketing tool. They have also produced several in-house books of their own. *StarGroup Spotlights* is a series of educational books produced by StarGroup International's Book Division.

This venture began as a philanthropic gesture by the company's president, Brenda Star, but unexpectedly sparked a demand that required a major effort to research, compile, and organize information to produce books on a variety of topics.

It started when Brenda, determined to entice parents to encourage their children to read instead of spending so much time in front of television sets, produced a book highlighting *101 Reasons To READ With Your Child*. StarGroup published 5,000 copies and donated them to Palm Beach County. Her philanthropic needs were satisfied ... or so she thought. Requests for copies were made from as far away as the states of Washington and Hawaii. Before long, requests for bulk orders began to arrive. A number of literacy advocates embraced it and the book was soon endorsed by such noted individuals as Art Linkletter, Mark Victor Hansen, successful Texas businessman and Horatio Alger recipient Tom Harken, and the late Dave Thomas among others. Demand for the book continued to grow, but StarGroup lacked the infrastructure to handle fulfillment of individual copies, and resources to underwrite large bulk press runs of additional printings. The book did go into a second printing in January 2001, when, at the request of Kentucky Governor Paul E. Patton, Toyota Motor Manufacturing of Kentucky underwrote the production for circulation among parents of young children in that state.

Then in September 2001 the shock that reverberated around the globe prompted Brenda to once again respond. The remarkable display of American unity following the 911 terrorist attacks, inspired Brenda and her associates to produce *101 Reasons To Be A Proud American.* StarGroup researched, drafted, designed, published, and had the book ready for distribution within six weeks of the tragedy.

It soon became evident that a trend was developing. While discussions about producing a book series were in progress, interest in the existing books continued to mount. Demands for more than a million copies have been received from across the country from Headstart Program teachers, schools, libraries, the National Alliance of Black Educators, and the Palm Beach County School System.

StarGroup determined that it was important to develop a series of educational books on a variety of topics in addition to Reading and American Patriotism. There are currently ten books in the *StarGroup Spotlights* series in print, ten more in development, and more being considered.

For the past two decades StarGroup International has met the needs of clients, ranging from Fortune 500 companies to local businesses and grass-roots organizations. StarGroup offers services in marketing, advertising, public relations, image development and book production.

By developing local, regional, national and international marketing campaigns, StarGroup International helps corporations, businesses, industries and a wide range of professionals send their message to target audiences.

For more information contact

StarGroup International at (561) 547-0667

or visit their website:

http://www.stargroupinternational.com